FROM WALL STREET
TO THE GREAT WALL

FROM WALL STREET TO THE GREAT WALL

How to Invest in China

JONATHAN WORRALL
PETER O'SHEA

Foreword by
Ivan Chung

John Wiley & Sons, Inc.

Published by John Wiley & Sons, Inc., Hoboken, New Jersey.
Published simultaneously in Canada.

For general information on our other products and services or for technical support, please contact our Customer Care Department within the United States at (800) 762-2974, outside the United States at (317) 572-3993 or fax (317) 572-4002.

Wiley also publishes its books in a variety of electronic formats. Some content that appears in print may not be available in electronic books. For more information about Wiley products, visit our web site at www.wiley.com.

ISBN-13 978-0-470-10911-3
ISBN-10 0-470-10911-4

Printed in the United States of America.

10 9 8 7 6 5 4 3 2 1

CONTENTS

FOREWORD:
INVESTING IN CHINA

IT IS not unusual for investors to complain about the reliability and quality of data about China, ranging from macroeconomic data to company financial statements. It is even less unusual for investors to be amazed at the spectacular growth in China, ranging from gross domestic product (GDP) to the value of an apartment in Shanghai. Apparently both are right.

Yet the massive flows of foreign direct investment (FDI) into China and increasing investments in overseas listed Chinese stocks (Warren Buffett's Berkshire Hathaway Inc., for example, owned 13.35 percent of the publicly traded shares in PetroChina at the time of writing) reveal that the second school of thought dominates. After all, lack of quality is not an issue unique to China but a generic issue with all emerging economies. What makes China a unique source of lucrative investment opportunities is its gigantic critical mass combined with its progressive migration to a market economy. In other words, investment success in China depends largely on the ability to diagnose and envision these two critical and dynamic driving forces. However, given China's limited transparency, relevant reliable research tools remain scarce. As such, the tools and research methodologies introduced in this book give investors an unparalleled edge to make sensible and well-informed investment decisions that can maximize their returns and minimize the risks.

China's economic reform started with the liberalization of its labor force and the progressive introduction of private property and foreign investment rights in and after 1979. The reform policies succeeded in mobilizing largely dormant labor and resources to economic production, thus substantially increasing the productive input to the economy. These reforms have been key drivers of the strong economic growth over the past 25 years.

Some China skeptics argue that the growth has been manipulated and is not real. There are indeed reasons to cast doubts on the validity and quality of some reported Chinese government data but, even so, the situation is improving. Furthermore, official data from China's trading and economic counterparts—U.S.-China trade deficit data, data on European Union FDI into China, China's holding of U.S. Treasuries figures, together with reexport figures from Hong Kong—provide solid evidence of China's sustained economic growth. A simple count of the number of television sets in Chinese households and automobiles on the roads proves that standards of living have improved substantially in both urban and rural areas in recent years.

Here begins the fascinating part of the investment research process. Under the backdrop of sustained economic growth and progressive migration to a more market-oriented economy, how does an investor pick the winners? What qualities do these winners have? Will current winners become tomorrow's losers?

As market forces become more and more prevalent, the range of variation among companies will become broader. Stronger companies have grasped the opportunities presented by market liberalization while weaker companies are losing market share as the support from the state fades out. But, according to our three years of experience in applying international standards to rating 180 Chinese companies, valuable research covers more than simple market factors and takes into account more considerations than we would cover in a developed market.

After all, China is still migrating to a full-fledged market economy. The true picture of the economy and of China's corporations is much more sophisticated and profound. First, control of shares of many corporations, including many listed companies, is still in state hands. Strategic sectors such as utilities, oil and gas, telecoms, aviation, and banking are dominated by state-controlled enterprises. In these areas, it is difficult to enhance disclosure and corporate governance and motivate the managers to be purely profit-oriented. Furthermore, prices of electricity, gasoline, cell phone services, air tickets, and interest rates are only partially liberalized and are still significantly regulated. Yet most upstream sectors like crude oil are already tracking global market prices. As a result, there are conflicts and pressures between upstream and downstream sectors of the economy. These sectors and most corporations within each sector are almost solely controlled by the state, making interest distribution among entities something that goes beyond economic logic. Thus, selecting winners is not straightforward and requires an understanding of China from the inside out and, more importantly, an ability to see and appreciate the dynamic changes in progress.

The following examples illustrate the point. Fueled by China's strong economic growth and huge population, there are now 300 million cell phone users (and still increasing), with service providers seeing fast-growing revenues. Yet China has only two mobile telecom service providers, with the dominant provider, China Mobile, enjoying a lucrative earnings before interest, taxes, depreciation, and amortization (EBITDA) margin of more than 55 percent. However, nearly all of China's 40-odd cell phone makers, most of which have entered the market in the past three years, are losing market share to Nokia, Motorola, and Samsung, and are suffering growing losses. Another example: While power shortages pushed electricity companies to increase their electricity output in 2005, driving up the price of coal, which follows global commodity prices, regulated tariffs increased only modestly during the period because of the corresponding socioeconomic impact. As a result, power companies reported substantial increases in revenues but reduced profit margins and net profit.

Even so, we believe that good investments in China present the same qualities as their counterparts in other countries: consistent delivery of growth in profitability, dividends, and returns to investors. These qualities mirror those of their international peers as leading Chinese companies become more and more active in the international capital markets and engage in cross-border acquisitions. Moreover, China's economy is becoming more and more liberalized and globalized—a trend that has been reinforced by a series of recent government policies, including the transformation of the previously rigid USD/RMB currency peg into a multicurrency peg with a wider trading band, as well as the implementation of a program to convert nontradable shares into tradable shares in listed state-owned enterprises.

With its valuable insight into the unique Chinese market and its credible guide to exploring Chinese companies, this book provides readers with a pioneering advantage, allowing them to grasp the lucrative opportunities in the Chinese market as its economy becomes increasingly market oriented.

In the years to come, the contribution of *From Wall Street to the Great Wall* to China's investment research landscape will be proven to be unprecedented, as China reforms itself to be one of the world's great economic powers.

IVAN CHUNG, CFA
Managing Director, Credit Ratings
Xinhua Finance
February 2006

ACKNOWLEDGMENTS

THIS BOOK is the result of a great deal of effort on the part of numerous people in the Xinhua Finance and Mergent family of companies. Not all of them can be thanked and acknowledged here. However, those whose contributions are particularly recognized include Ivan Chung, Managing Director of Xinhua Finance's Credit Ratings Division; Zhu Shan, Managing Director of Xinhua Finance's Indices Division; and Graham Earnshaw, Editor-in-Chief of *Xinhua Finance News*. Of particular note were the efforts by Michael C. Thomsett, whose meticulous research and knowledge made a huge contribution to this project. Thanks are also due to the staff of Mergent and Xinhua Finance, whose diligent efforts in compiling data and research also contributed to this project.

INTRODUCTION:
THE NEW FACE OF
WORLD ECONOMICS

J OB MIGRATION. Shortages of skilled workers. Competition within industries. All these symptoms of growth tell us something. Growth comes in a variety of shapes and sizes, but when we see it occurring along with emergence of technological and skilled levels of manufacturing, it is significant.

Historically dominated by an agricultural population, China today is undergoing a vast migration, not only in the sense of where people live, but also the types of jobs they hold and seek, their wages, and the entire economic viewpoint among working people and industry. Many nonagricultural manufacturing sectors in China are growing in double digits each year as the country's industrial economy explodes.

In this environment, the country struggles with the problems typical of an emerging economic base: the need for improved training programs, unemployment, energy demand, and housing. But the problem is not what to do with a labor force; the problem is competition among industrialized cities within China to attract young workers. In 2005, a major manufacturing center in South China, Shenzhen, found only 53,000 applicants for 105,000 skilled technician openings. The city estimates demand for more than two million skilled workers over a five-year period beginning in 2005. Shanghai, another center with a growing demand for skilled workers, anticipates similar problems filling jobs in the future.[1]

This explosion in skilled jobs has positive ramifications for investors, both in China and elsewhere in the world. The lack of skilled labor is certainly an impediment to growth, but as growth pangs go, it is a more desirable problem than the alternative, a lack of available jobs for existing skilled workers. As the country works to adjust to the ever-growing demand levels in skilled vocations, advance company training programs and investment, and manage a population shifting toward industrialized areas, investors from the United States and other trading partners of China may realize the investment potential within Chinese industry, on many fronts.

For investors outside China, the problem is in determining how to invest capital in a range of promising industries, not only technology and manufacturing, but many others as well. China's growth is rapid and occurring across many investment sectors. Investors who understand this growth curve may want to be involved, but do not know how to go about moving capital from traditional western markets to the massive and ever-expanding Asian economy.

This book presents an overview of the current situation, the background, and the potential for investment in China and in its potentially lucrative industries. Equally important, the book provides suggestions for exactly how capital can be invested without having to move funds overseas. In many countries, including the United States, the complexity of opening accounts in foreign countries, working with stock exchange rules dissimilar to their domestic exchanges, and managing risks is simply too extensive. As a consequence, many investors who desire multinational asset allocation or who recognize the potential in China's market have simply decided that, without more knowledge, it is not prudent to attempt to move funds into that market.

This book shows you how you can invest directly in China's emerging growth boom—without the complexity and risk associated with investing overseas. Using domestic outlets, you can become an international investor. This book explains not only how to move money into the Asian market safely and easily; it also provides you with vast resources for analysis and identification of profitable companies and industries.

As the opportunities continue to present themselves for investment in a dynamic and growing economy, you will find many ways to put capital to good use. The growth pains identified by the symptoms of skilled-labor shortages and competition among industrial areas are problems, of course; however, they also serve as symptoms of strongly positive change. These problems are typical in growing and productive economies.

We present information to you in two sections of this book. Part I, A Premise for a New World View, demonstrates how China is emerging as the leading economic power in the twenty-first century. As the world becomes truly global in economic terms, a variety of shifts must be expected to occur. Agricultural, manufacturing, high-tech, medical, and research industries— among others, of course—are already shifting away from traditionally dominant economies in North America and Europe toward China, India, and other Asian growth centers. Part I shows how and why this is occurring. The shift in economic and monetary influence is both rapid and profound; the implications of these changes are as significant as the Industrial Revolution was in Europe of the past; and new developments will change the way that workers function within the economy of each region or country. For example, in the future, the primary competition may not be between the United States and Asia as a whole, but between China and India *within* the larger Asian market. The potential for changes such as this affects every investor in every country. Along with changes in centers of economic influence come changes in investment opportunities.

In Part II, Methods and Strategies in the New Market, you will discover exactly how China is growing and which industries are the strongest. Like all economic centers, the Chinese economy is partially self-reliant and partially dependent on outside resources. The growing population and manufacturing base of China will make it the future's leading energy-buying nation. In the past, the United States held this role; but changes in economic as well as in demographic realities will also change the relative demand base for natural resources.

China faces many challenges in its promising future. Although you as an investor can observe a lot from the economic situation in that country, you also need to be able to assess the situation from a new perspective. In the western world, growth has usually been associated with labor *shortages*. In China today, there is no shortage of unskilled labor, but there is fierce competition for skilled workers in the fastest-growing sectors, primarily technology. The challenge of gearing up to better train people to fill skilled jobs is huge, and it is difficult to imagine in terms of time, investment, and social changes. At the same time, China also needs to balance its industrial needs with the equally important needs of its agrarian base. There are, in fact, two Chinas in this respect. The heavily industrialized China and the agricultural segment are separated in many respects. Income levels and requirements, employment, poverty, geography, and cultural priorities are among these; also of great importance is the challenge to China of how it balances the priorities of industrialized and agricultural population groups.

Investors who are aware of these cultural and social forces will be well equipped to determine exactly how their investment resources can be put to work. Although foreign investors will normally funnel their capital through domestic outlets—and appropriately so—it is not enough to simply trust an adviser. In the United States, for example, history has shown that advice is not always sound, nor is it given in the best interests of the investor. Most experienced investors have discovered, often at great expense, that they need to be very selective and critical of the advice they receive and act upon. This has not changed.

In this book, you are provided with resources you can use to perform your own research or to locate and maximize information provided by objective research outlets. However, decisions invariably are better made with high-quality research. This book is not intended to make research easier; it is designed to help you focus your research efforts intelligently, so that you will be able to avoid the common problems investors face in any specialized plan. This includes investing in specialized or risky products, unfamiliar industries, or foreign countries. The resources you find in this book will help you to identify the risk elements you need to be aware of, and to make informed decisions based on objective research. As with any investment plan, this is a sensible formula for reducing risk and finding out how to protect capital.

As a potential investor in Chinese growth, you face the usual challenges every investor faces: identifying opportunities, matching appropriate risks, and proceeding through the appropriate venue. You also face the additional challenges of a dissimilar culture and social order. This book helps you to understand these aspects of your investment decisions, and to improve your knowledge of this new and promising market.

PART I

A PREMISE FOR A NEW WORLD VIEW

CHAPTER 1

AN ECONOMIC HISTORY OF CHINA

IMAGINE A city growing from undeveloped countryside to an urban center the size of Chicago—in less than 15 years. Add to this a financial district eight times larger than London's, and you have Shanghai today.

China's economy is the fastest growing in the world. This is true not only in terms of increased production, manufacturing, and exports, but also in monetary position. As of 2005, China was the second largest investor in foreign exchange reserves, consisting primarily of U.S. dollars. These changes can be viewed as upsetting to the order and priority of things or as an opportunity for new investment in the twenty-first century.

This economic growth is not taking place in a third world nation by any means (in spite of a persistent image held by many westerners). China has more than 200 million people considered middle class. And although this large nation consists of many dissimilar economic regions, China is clearly an industrialized country, at least in its geographically industrialized areas. With this status come numerous problems, as anyone would expect. Other nations have suffered economic and cultural shifts in periods of expansion and they have overcome those problems in time. China's case will be no different, and the numbers tell the story. Annual investment in fixed assets and infrastructure runs at $600 billion a year or about 40 percent of the country's $1.5 trillion gross domestic product (GDP).[1]

In this chapter, you will find a western perspective on the China phenomenon—a view of economic and cultural history based on events that have occurred worldwide, in Europe, and in the United States, and how those important key periods in history have created the modern environment. Finally, you will see how and why the next evolutionary step in this historical trend is unavoidably global, and why China will play a dominant role in coming years.

ECONOMIC TRENDS AND ENERGY DEMAND

Western investors need to educate themselves about China, and they need to put aside misconceptions and outdated ideas about what exactly defines China and the Asian economy. For the past century, the United States has collectively assumed that it would always remain the leader in terms of world economic might. In comparison, China has dreamed of an unlimited market for its manufactured goods. The U.S. dream may prove more elusive than anybody thought and, in fact, the U.S. investor may need to scramble to rethink the global ramifications of how and where to invest.

For China, the dream of an expanded world market is coming to pass, but not necessarily as an exporter. In the past, the Chinese perspective saw the rest of the world (especially the United States) as a buyer. Today, China has emerged as a competitive force in imports as well. However, no form of growth continues without limitations, and the greatest threat to continued economic expansion in China involves finite energy supplies. China requires tremendous natural resources to run its expanding manufacturing base, and the Chinese worker wants to have an automobile, 24-hour utilities, and other benefits enjoyed by China's industrialized neighbors. The scope of recent growth in China is immense. In 1980, when the nation was only beginning to emerge as a serious economic competitor to the United States and European economies, its overall exports were a mere $13 billion per year. By 2003, exports had grown to $450 billion.[2]

Of course, growth is never easy and never occurs without consequences. China's population is 1.3 billion, four times greater than the United States. Exports to the United States have grown 415 percent in 15 years.[3] Accompanying this is growth in domestic demand within China, which today is the world's second largest consumer of energy and third largest importer of oil—causing, at least to some extent, the rising oil prices domestically as well as internationally. The domestic demand is not restricted to industry, either. As Chinese families experience ever-improving standards of living, they want more material goods as well: home ownership, automobiles, and more. All these growing demands place a strain on an economy already struggling to meet current demand, not always successfully. On the basis of energy demand alone, China's demand is not being met currently and the situation becomes increasingly difficult as more growth creates, in turn, higher levels of demand for energy.

China not only is importing its needed resources, but it also mines its own resources at home. For example, China has become the world's largest producer of coal and may also be involved in the development of new energy technologies as demand continues to grow. These new developments include the innovation of so-called clean coal. One big problem with traditional methods of coal consumption is the environmental impact it causes. Today 75 percent of China's 400,000-megawatt demand comes from coal, which, when consumed in the traditional manner, causes severe environmental pollution. A new clean-coal technology (CCT) is being developed in China as well as in the United States. It is a technology involving *coal liquefaction*, a system in which coal is crushed and combined with hydrogen and other liquids, creating a clean-burning and highly efficient synthetic oil. This liquid coal is more efficient to transport than solid coal, it burns clean, and it is not expensive to produce. The liquid version of coal is essential to China because its industry is in the far south, but most of its mining operations are in the north. The problem of moving coal from mine to factory is so severe that, even with its large coal reserves, China imports coal from other countries. Liquefaction technology could facilitate movement of coal quickly and cheaply by pipeline to meet growing demand, without adding significant costs.

China's energy requirements are severe and will only get worse unless new technology is developed and put into use. Today, Chinese factories and homes experience many problems with electrical power, including blackouts and brownouts during peak usage hours. This problem will impede future growth if new technologies are not developed soon.

Demand for power and resources (including alternative energy) presents tremendous investment opportunities, as well as social and political problems for China. The anticipated growth in the region may be inhibited if energy and natural resources cannot keep up with the expansion itself. China—like the United States—is facing chronic shortages that affect not only homes but factories, too. Electrical power shortages are chronic today. Blackouts are not uncommon, and manufacturing is affected directly.

Consider the parallel to the United States in the nineteenth century. During the U.S. expansion, booming industrial centers created the same environmental and energy problems and, with coal as a primary source of energy—just like in China today—the very definition of an expanding industrial economy invariably has to involve interim environmental and energy problems.

It is difficult for consumers outside of China to imagine the real costs of energy gaps. However, consider the effect of a similar problem in the United States, where, beyond the mere inconvenience of lost power, the costs are staggering:

> In Manhattan, the skyline is dark . . . elevators freeze between floors . . . hospital machines give their last blip . . . and in the press rooms, computer terminals go black . . . in California, the world's fifth largest economy, the same happens over and over again. . . .
>
> Maybe 29 hours in the dark sounds like nothing to you. But when it happened in 2003, New York alone lost about $1.05 billion . . . or around $36 million per hour. Workers couldn't work. Tourists couldn't shop. Markets and restaurants couldn't keep food cold. Even the marquees on Broadway and the neon on Times Square went black. And it wasn't just New York. In Michigan, where a few of America's cars are still made, losses from the same power outage piled up to $691 million.[4]

If U.S. losses are $36 million per hour in a 29-hour blackout, it does not take much imagination to anticipate similar big-scale losses in a country with a larger population, a growing manufacturing base, and ever-greater energy demand.

So there exists a duality: a problem associated with industrial growth *and* an immediate investment opportunity. To the extent that Chinese utility corporations (whether state owned or independent) recognize the growing demand, investors will profit by identifying the opportunities to participate. Infrastructure demands capital; and, as the experience of nineteenth-century America proves, it requires a lot of capital, which ultimately leads to profits. Investment in infrastructure is not permanent, however. As you will see later in this book, the experience in the United States proved that investment opportunities—even in infrastructure—are temporary. The era of massive infrastructure investment in the United States has passed, but a similar area of economic growth and expansion in China is only just beginning.

No growth curve lasts forever, and many factors may inhibit that growth. The critical point has already arrived in China, and alternate sources or types of energy are needed today. This was explained in an article examining the relationship between energy requirements and factory production:

> China's economic boom is, quite literally, running out of power. Since 1980, when the nation's economy first began to emerge from the darkness, energy consumption has skyrocketed by more than 150 percent. But construction of new power plants has not kept pace.[5]

Putting it another way, the continuation of industrial growth—and related jobs and training, economic health, environmental safety, productivity, trade balances, standards of living, and competitive forces—is going to depend on identifying energy sources to keep up with the growing demand. If the established western view—dependence on Middle East oil—is the position to be accepted in China, known world reserves will run out by 2030, based on current usage levels. Other sources of energy and fuel must be developed, and in the near future, or growth—not only in China, but worldwide—will not be able to continue at present levels.

The problem is not unique to China, of course. Energy shortages also occur in the United States, for example, where blackouts big enough to affect a half million homes occur with regularity, every four months on average.[6] The solution, according to President Bush in a 2005 address, is to fund and develop alternative sources of energy to offset growing demand:

> The first essential step toward greater energy independence is to apply technology to increase domestic production from existing energy resources. And one of the most promising sources of energy is nuclear power. Today's technology has made nuclear

power safer, cleaner, and more efficient than ever before. Nuclear power is now providing about 20 percent of America's electricity, with no air pollution or greenhouse gas emissions. Nuclear power is one of the safest, cleanest sources of power in the world. . . .[7]

The same arguments apply in China, where energy production has also increased. The safety and low environmental impact of modern nuclear power compared to other sources make this one of the more promising sources for future energy production. From an investor's point of view, this reality makes China-based corporations that are involved in the nuclear industry promising investment opportunities in the near future. The Chinese development of this technology has already begun; by the beginning of 2005, the country had a total of 43 operational nuclear power plants, and the trend continues:

China is on the biggest power-plant building spree the world has ever seen. Last year spending on generators almost doubled to 200 billion yuan. So many new hydroelectric dams, coal-fired generators and nuclear facilities are being built, the equivalent of Britain's entire electricity output is being added to the capacity of the country's national grid every two years. . . .[8]

The modern version of nuclear technology is a far cry from power plants of the past. New techniques based on hydrogen fission are safer, are more economical, and offer the potential for unimaginable sources of new energy with none of the dangers. This technology may be the answer, for China as well as for the United States, to the chronic problems of dependence on Middle East oil. For example, 30 grams of hydrogen can provide the same energy as 100,000 gallons of gasoline. This new version of nuclear-based energy resource is not unique to the United States; it also provides incredible potential in China. New power plants, utilizing new sources of nuclear power, are likely to provide answers to future world energy consumption. Dependence on the Middle East (where high technology is rare and no coal reserves are to be found) will run its course before the middle of this century, and world industrial powers will run their plants and their cities on nuclear-based power sources. The U.S.-based development is aptly described in the following passage:

> The hydrogen economy is really a nuclear economy. Investors and the rest of corporate America may not realize how close the country is to making a gigantic bet on a nuclear future. . . . We are talking about literally thousands of new nuclear facilities dedicated to the production of hydrogen through fission powered electrolysis (the splitting of water into hydrogen and oxygen gas).[9]

These emerging fuel innovations are exciting from a Chinese as well as from a U.S. perspective. The nuclear and coal technologies known today to be possible will revolutionize the entire energy sector, a point worth keeping in mind for investors. Future energy demand may well be met by China and the United States to the exclusion of the Middle East. Both countries have vast coal resources as yet unmined and, of great interest, the Middle East has no such reserves whatsoever. Investors who grasp the ramifications of these developments will be especially keen on locating ways to invest capital in companies likely to be on the cutting edge of new energy technology, both in the West and in China.

The observation that future energy needs must change is not mere speculation. From now until 2030, estimates are that the world will need to invest a half trillion dollars *per year* just to keep up with current demand—and not even allowing for *increased* demand.[10]

Although the United States and other industrialized nations in North America and Europe are keenly aware of the coming energy crunch, they are not alone. China is growing rapidly, and its energy needs are in many ways more critical than those of the rest of the world. A comparison to past history makes the point.

COMPARISONS IN HISTORY

The changes under way in the world economy are no subtle shift in emphasis. There is a tendency to ignore current events because it is difficult to comprehend the significance of singular changes for the future. Today's changes are technological and economic, but they will have as much impact on how the world will look half a century from now as did the major turning points of the past. In western history, the events that shaped who and what the world looks like today include both catastrophes and positive events, such as the fourteenth-century Black Death, the sixteenth-century Age of Discovery, and the eighteenth- and nineteenth-century Industrial Revolution.

These represent major and significant adjustments in the economic world balance. The current era is comparable—for many reasons—to other periods in history in the scope and importance of how it will affect our lives. From a western perspective, events and period trends have defined how *western* economic forces have been shaped. Today, the same trend is taking place, but it will occur worldwide. From a strictly western perspective, several important periods have not only influenced economic events, they have created them.

The Fourteenth-Century Black Death, Worldwide

In the year A.D. 1347, the Black Death struck Europe, and over the following three years between one-third and one-half of Europe's population died. This single event had devastating results for the next 400 years. Shortages of labor prevented the European economy from growing until the Industrial Revolution and mechanization of industry. The Black Death was not restricted to Europe; in fact, it was more likely a worldwide pandemic, with infection spreading from travelers using the trade routes (the Silk Road, among others). Years before the European outbreak, in the 1330s, the plague struck in the Chinese province of Hubei. Again in the 1350s and following the European plague years, China suffered plague in at least eight districts: Hubei, Jiangxi, Shanxi, Hunan, Guangdong, Guangxi, Henan, and Suiyuan.[11]

The plague spread from Italy throughout all of Europe and also to the Middle East and Egypt. As catastrophic as the immediate effects were of the plague, the consequences in terms of population (thus, labor) were felt worldwide for centuries after the plague years. In the 1334 outbreak in Hubei, estimates claim that *90 percent* of the population was lost to the plague. Two-thirds of China's entire population may have passed away two decades later, in the 1353–1354 era. The same was true in the European experience, where some 25 million deaths occurred. Many areas were completely depopulated as a result, with larger urban areas harder hit due to the easy spread of the disease.

The loss of population had immediate and long-lasting economic effect and was one of the most significant events in world history. For example, labor shortages gave workers greater power and the ability to demand higher wages. Population levels, already cut by the plague, continued to fall for the next 100 years in Europe and caused economic slowdown, population mobility, and economic as well as social chaos. The move away from serfdom and toward the Renaissance has been attributed by some historians to the Black Death. However, it is difficult in modern times to know with any degree of certainty whether the plagues hitting the world in the fourteenth century had a common root and to what degree those catastrophes affected future events.

Imagine the immediate effects of a continent-wide health crisis. In Europe following the plague years, construction projects were not finished, debtors died without making repayment, and normal commerce ceased because people were afraid to congregate. Craftsmen and artisans died, so essential work on many levels did not go forward. Labor shortages had conflicting results: Although workers had more power to demand higher wages, landlords tightened their hold on serfs. In many areas, crops went untended, leading to widespread food shortages and famines. Social chaos caused complete disintegration in many areas, both socially and economically. The plague led to decades of guild revolts and outright rebellion (for example, the Jacquerie in 1358, the Peasants' Revolt in 1381, and the Catalonian Rebellion in 1395).

The plague years remain one of the periods in European history that not only marked a turning point in the social order, but affected events until the eighteenth century and, in many respects, beyond.

The Age of Discovery—the Fifteenth Century

Two hundred years after Europe was economically destroyed by the Black Death, the continent's population began to grow once again. The economy also improved. Europeans began looking to other parts of the world and envisioning both trade and conquest as possible paths to world power and wealth. The late fifteenth century was a period of strong growth in mercantilism and the desire for colonial influence in Asia, Africa, and the Americas.

This period in western history was the first example of the creation of a global economy. For centuries, Europe had traded with the Far East across the vast stretches of Eastern Europe, the Middle East, and Asia. The Silk Road (from the German *Seidenstrasse*, a term first used in the nineteenth century in Germany and coined by

Ferdinand von Richthofen) connected Chang'an, China, to Middle Eastern and European destinations, both by land and by sea. The overland route, over 7,000 miles, stretched from coastal areas of North China on the Pacific Ocean through to the Mediterranean Sea. Using camels and horses as far back as 4,000 B.C., traders used the Silk Road to its maximum extent by the first century B.C. after efforts led by China to open trade with India and the western world. The sea route began in the Chinese province of Jiaozhi (known to-day as Vietnam), with ports in India as well as Egypt and other ports along the northern stretches of the Red Sea.

Trade occurring along land and sea routes known collectively as the Silk Road was primarily commercial; it was also a form of cul-tural exchange. In the late thirteenth century, Italian Marco Polo traveled to China and created both curiosity and commercial inter-est throughout Europe. Two hundred years later, European mer-chants had an effect not only on profits for both regions, but also on cultural, political, and social change. However, there was a problem: To travel the distance from western Europe to the far western areas of China took months and was costly as well. The entire premise be-hind the European Age of Discovery was motivated by a desire to find a faster route to the Far East. At the time, no one realized how large the world was; the existence of the American continents and the Pacific Ocean was not widely known. The few people who were aware of the American continents had no idea how large they were, nor did they realize the vastness of the Pacific Ocean.

In spite of popular myth stating that people of the fifteenth century believed the earth to be flat, it was simply not the case. Scholars of the fifteenth century realized that the earth was round, meaning it was possible that a faster sea route to China and India could be discovered. (The origin of the term "Indian" as applied to American tribes grew from the fact that Columbus believed at the conclusion of his first voyage that he had arrived in India.)

During this period, when European nations—finally begin-ning to recover economically from the loss of population and economic growth from two centuries before—began expanding their colonial interests, the economic advantages of finding a route to the Far East by traveling by sea in a westward direction was compelling. Thus, the Age of Discovery, as it has been called, was not originally designed as a discovery program at all, but a program with economic incentives. The creation of a worldwide trading economy affected economic conditions as widely as the Black Death had two centuries before.

To western societies, the voyages of Christopher Columbus starting in 1492 are the best-known. Columbus's voyages were the beginning of a trend lasting decades. Following Columbus were explorers like John and Sabastian Cabot (Italians who landed in Labrador in 1497), who were sent by England's King Henry VII to find a northwest passage to India—a goal that was never realized and was motivated by lack of knowledge of world geography.

In 1499, Italian Amerigo Vespucci also explored westward. (Vespucci first mapped America and the continent was named after him.) Also exploring South America was Vincent Yanez Pinson, who located the mouth of the Amazon River. Later explorers such as Juan Ponce de Leon and Hernando Cortez further opened up the American continents, but without discovering a faster route to China or India. The Age of Discovery did not attain the original goals of cutting the time required to reach China, but it did uncover a vast new two-continent area in the Americas. The original belief was that the world was much smaller than its 24,900-mile girth. Although there was no shorter route to the Far East, the rich resources of the Americas changed Europe's economy and culture forever.

In a sense, the economic necessity for reducing travel time between China and Europe defined the fifteenth century, even though the original goal was never realized. That goal had been to accumulate riches and make trade more efficient, but the accidental benefit was the expansion of European influence throughout the world. The recognition of the importance of trade with China foreshadowed the trend under way today, in the twenty-first century.

English Civil War, Precursor to the Industrial Revolution

In chronicling events, either positive or negative, that have set the course of the western economy, we cannot ignore the significance of the Industrial Revolution. All of history consists of a series of stepping stones, one leading to the other. So we cannot study the Industrial Revolution without understanding how other events in western economic history led up to those times. And, of course, we cannot understand the modern global ramifications of change without also understanding how such an important change occurred.

The Industrial Revolution took place in England during the eighteenth and nineteenth centuries. The era began with the discovery of steam power and, as a result, automation of machinery, notably in agriculture and the textile industry. In addition, steam power was revolutionary. Its industrial application changed all modes of transportation, enabling the efficient development of shipping and rail travel, not only in Europe but also in the United States. By the nineteenth century, steam power was largely responsible for the success of the U.S. westward expansion, often referred to as the Second Industrial Revolution.

The economic trends associated with the Industrial Revolution grew directly from social changes that started 400 years earlier, after the Black Death. That catastrophe made labor a valuable commodity, perhaps for the first time. Thus, while landlords tried to tighten their hold on serfs to replace agricultural workers lost to the plague, skilled craftsmen were able to demand more wage and benefit concessions. It was the state of feudalism and the changes that that institution went through that led, indirectly, to the Industrial Revolution.

A turning point in European history was a series of civil wars occurring in the seventeenth century. Known collectively as the English Civil War, there were actually three phases involved and, in historical perspective, these wars were the gateway from a largely feudal system to the complete removal of the landlord/serf dynamic, which in turn paved the way for the Industrial Revolution.

The first, called the Bishop's War, was fought in 1639 and 1640. The English and Scots fought over attempts by English King Charles I to reform the church. The Scots opposed reform and wanted to remove civil power from the Anglican bishops. Charles gathered an army and attacked Scotland without adequate funding and without support from Parliament.

The Bishop's War went nowhere. But between 1642 and 1651 a series of new civil wars renewed the struggle. The first stretched from 1642 to 1646. The conflict in this instance was between Charles I and the English Parliament. Charles left London after a failed attempt at arresting parliamentary members who did not agree with him; the war proceeded along class and geographic lines. Royalist support for Charles I was located in the north, west, and Wales; the wealthier southern and eastern areas of England supported Parliament. By 1646, Charles had depleted his resources, and he fled north to Scotland. A second civil war lasted from 1647 to 1651, again with forces aligned either with the king or with Parliament. In 1648, the Scots invaded England but were defeated. In 1649 Charles was tried by Parliament, found guilty of treason, and beheaded. Oliver Cromwell was appointed by Parliament to restore order and, in 1651, he defeated the invading Scots and was named Lord Protector of England.

As is often the case in civil wars, neither side was able to win decisively, causing the conflict to go on for many years—in this instance for 12 years. Admittedly, characterizing the English Civil War as merely a conflict between king and Parliament does not tell the whole story. In many respects, it was a social and cultural revolution as well. Just as the U.S. Civil War of the nineteenth century had the result of ending slavery, shifting economic power, and consolidating the political center of the nation, there were also numerous social and economic causes for the war itself; no one issue caused the outbreak of armed conflict. It is invariably the case. In England, another form of slavery—the feudal system—was one of many issues leading to the 12-year series of conflicts. This period is critical to western culture today because it resulted in the end of the feudal system, making it possible for the Industrial Revolution to commence soon after.

The cultural and social disruptions of civil war are well known in China as well. In the Han Dynasty (A.D. 206–220), extended internal military conflict led to creation of the Three Kingdoms. These were the three major economic regions under the Han Dynasty, and they were named Wei (northern China), Shu (west), and Wu (east). These approximate kingdoms are illustrated in Figure 1.1.

Continous civil war followed in an attempt by Ts'ao Ts'ao, ruler of the strongest Wei kingdom, to unite these separate kingdoms into a single nation. Wei and Shu merged and became a single kingdom in A.D. 263. Under the Tang Dynasty (618–907) the country was consolidated and China enjoyed peace and prosperity, controlled the Silk Road, and witnessed an age in which innovation and culture (including Buddhism) flourished throughout the nation.

Over many hundreds of years, China has experienced numerous internal conflicts but nothing else as major as the twentieth-century civil war. In the first half of that century, British influence led to a devastating division of Chinese territory among several European colonial powers. In the 1930s a massive conflict between the National Revolutionary Army in southern China under Sun Yatsen and the Chinese Communist Party under Mao Zedong created utter and long-lasting chaos. An added

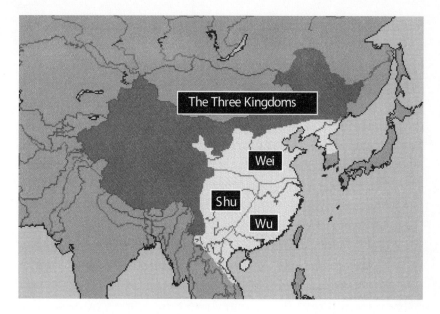

FIGURE 1.1　THE THREE CHINESE KINGDOMS

invasion of Manchuria by Japan in 1931 preceded Japan's domination of most of China during World War II. Finally, in 1949, the People's Republic of China was made official, ending decades of war and turmoil.

Just as the English Civil War led to the Industrial Revolution in the West, the Chinese civil wars of the twentieth century preceded the modern economic revolution that is accelerating into the twenty-first century. The parallel is unmistakable.

The Industrial Revolution of the Eighteenth and Nineteenth Century in England

The concept of any revolution is associated with great social upheaval and change. This has been true in England, China, the United States, and virtually anywhere else a revolution has occurred. The English Civil War of the seventeenth century led immediately to the Industrial Revolution, a striking parallel to the way that economic events are leading today to an economic revolution around the world that is, notably, being led by China.

The end of English feudalism was one of the primary causes of the cultural and social changes during these years. Developments in technology, food production, textile manufacturing, and transportation (based on developments of steam power and automation of machinery) affected not only labor markets but financial markets as well, both in England and with all of the country's trading partners. As an economic revolution, these events occurred in England rather than elsewhere because of the advances in social structure. Under a feudal system (such as that existing in France and Germany into the seventeenth and eighteenth centuries) parochial interests inhibited any national trends in markets. Locally imposed tariffs, for example, prevented trade within nations as well as with foreign interests. In England, a unified national market enabled the country to pursue international trade on a large scale, as well as develop its military and naval power, expand colonial interests, and control trade in many commodities (including tobacco, alcohol, and slavery, for example).

Steam power is normally associated with this period in relation to agriculture, transportation, and textiles. However, another effect was equally important: Steam-powered printing methods led to production of a vastly expanded number of books and periodicals, which in turn improved English literacy. Informed citizens demanded increased rights, not only in England but in the American colonies as well. High literacy caused greater involvement in political processes, a major cause for the American Revolutionary War with England.

Textile industries in England were, until early in the eighteenth century, based on the use of wool that was processed by hand by artisans. This cottage industry (so named because textile artisans performed spinning and weaving out of their homes) was the mainstay of textiles until two important changes occurred. First, cotton imported from America replaced wool as the primary material (and America also displaced India as the major cotton supplier to England). Second, innovations in production led to more efficient, cheaper methods in textiles, from spinning to rolling. Output increased as new machines were put into use (with mechanized looms replacing spinning wheels and hand looms), and, ultimately, the whole industry was mechanized.

The United States experienced an industrial revolution of its own during the nineteenth century. (In Chapter 2, you will see how the expansion of the United States and its investment in national infrastructure parallels today's similar social trends in China.)

Why did the Industrial Revolution take place in England with a second phase taking place in the United States rather than China? Many theories have put been forth by historians. Among the most likely is the theory offered by historian and author Kenneth Pommerantz, who has observed that while Europe and China were very similar in 1700, England's abundant and available natural resources made all the difference. England also had the ability to import natural resources from a huge colonial empire; thus the country was able to grow economically and as a world power.[12]

Another theory has been advanced that at the time of the Industrial Revolution China was in a "high level equilibrium trap," one in which manual agricultural methods were efficient enough that there was no perceived need for improvements. Thus, mechanization did not occur because there was no urgency to create the change.[13]

THE ECONOMIC REVOLUTION IN CHINA TODAY

The picture has changed drastically. It might have been true 300 years ago that there was no compelling reason for China to undergo an industrial revolution. Today, though, the demand for an economic revolution is quite urgent, and the need for change does exist.

In historical perspective, the Industrial Revolution was primarily based in agricultural developments, transportation, and manufacturing. The changes themselves made it possible for populations to expand. Following the Black Death 400 years earlier, the European continent had adjusted to food production, manufacturing, and cultural survival based on postplague population levels. The Industrial Revolution may have come about as a result of England's desire to expand as a world power; it also provides the means by which the revolution itself was made *affordable* in England.

The same argument can be made about China today and the new global economic revolution. In the last 30 years of the twentieth century, China changed as much as England changed in the 200 years leading up to the Industrial Revolution. Major cities in China grew from small towns into major metropolitan centers with high-rise buildings, automobiles, and highly specialized technology (and the labor market to go along with it). As much as anywhere else in the world, China is automated with computers, cell phones, digital technology, and more. Transportation, both for import and for export, has radically changed the way China operates. The innovation of the enclosed shipping container changed shipping everywhere in the world, but especially in China.

Just as English citizens of post-feudal England demanded better wages, improved working conditions, freedom from forced apprenticeship, and higher wages, the Chinese worker of today is also making demands. Wages for specialized technological jobs are high, and China is suffering a shortage of qualified, trained people to fill them. In China today, the government faces two problems concerning the labor force. First, high unemployment among unskilled workers and those with only an agricultural background will not be solved overnight, and advanced, accelerated training programs are needed to upgrade the skill levels of these workers. Second, if anything is likely to stunt China's growth, it will be the lack of skilled workers accompanied by a chronic energy crisis in China's expanding economy. Chinese government estimates indicate a demand for

600,000 engineers and scientists *per year*, while China-based universities and technical schools are able to supply less than one-third of that demand.[14]

There can be little doubt that these social and economic challenges will be confronted and overcome, both in China and globally. Today, the world faces an increasing interdependence in economic terms on trading partners and past enemies alike. Monetary exchange rates are tied together today more than ever before; for example, China's central bank is quickly becoming the world's largest holder of U.S. Treasury securities. Trends such as this make the point: No country can expect to assume the role of a competitive industrial power without also working together with other nations.

This makes the China story an exciting one, not only for modern historians and social scientists, but for investors as well. Every problem and every social movement involves serious problems that have to be overcome, as well as incredible investment opportunities. This requires that you become aware of the opportunities and then figure out how to gain information.

CHAPTER 2

WORLDWIDE CHANGE AND THE GLOBALIZATION OF INVESTMENTS

"CHANGE IS constant."[1] It is inevitable and unavoidable. Progress grows out of change, even though a host of problems occur during periods of change. Today the world is in the middle of one of the most significant economic changes in history.

This change contains several aspects. Among these is the overused but accurate concept of *globalization*. With instant cell phone and Internet access from and to everyone else, it is impossible to ignore the reality: You are in touch for the first time, instantly and affordably, with the rest of the world. As an investor, you probably realize what this means: It no longer makes sense to invest only in your home country, because strong markets are going to shift continually; cannot be expect to exist only at home; and, by definition, are going to expand over more than one country, region, or continent.

In the U.S. markets of the past, cyclical movement and sector strength were known to shift in a predictable pattern, and industry-specific investing was a widely practiced and logical strategy—assuming timing was usually right. The economic cycles of investing continue to apply today. During the 1980s and 1990s the idea of investing in foreign countries became the rage, especially in the mutual fund business. In those days, the idea of global funds or funds devoted to a specific country or continent was a novelty. And the idea caught on.

Interestingly, funds designed to seek profits overseas did not necessarily outperform U.S. markets on a consistent basis. The initial selling point was that some overseas markets were better than domestic markets. Although this is true at times, it is not always the case. The American investor has discovered that, just as U.S. sectors go through cycles, so do international markets. It's the same rule of thumb, but observed on a global scale. Investors today need to view foreign countries (as well as specific sectors) in the same way that U.S. sectors were viewed in the past. The popularity of investing internationally as a novel idea has to take on a realistic connotation. Today, it is not just a fanciful way to achieve asset allocation; it has become a necessity.

CHANGES IN ECONOMIC GEOGRAPHY

Just as sectors gain and lose strength and popularity in predictable trends—investment cycles—the economic geography shifts as well. Every investor is aware that there have been various ages in history in which different countries and continents exerted world domination and influence. England was a colonial and military power from the fifteenth century to the nineteenth century, and other European countries—Italy, Spain, Germany, Portugal, Belgium, Holland, and France, for example—have all experienced eras of military might and mercantile wealth derived from colonial expansion. In the Middle Ages, the Roman Church enjoyed an extended period of European domination, in which it served the dual roles of church and temporal power. Its influence was traced back to the alliance between the Roman

Empire and the Church, leading to creation of the *Roman Catholic Church* and its world leadership, during which it controlled the European economy and led wars (crusades) while holding influence over people's lives.

Today's economic power may not look the same as it did 1,000 years ago. Historically, however, power and influence have shifted from one region to another. The United States established itself as a world power during the nineteenth century when it expanded westward to become a two-ocean continental nation. Europe first took the United States seriously as a world power early in the century when the United States established itself as a naval power in the Atlantic Ocean and Mediterranean Sea and after the War of 1812 (which was anything but a clear-cut victory for either side, but which established the place of the United States in the world). In a sense, setting up a military presence goes hand in hand with establishing trading rights, as each country's history has demonstrated in turn.

The economic geography in China has also experienced periods of expansion and contraction. The twenty-first century is shaping up as the Asian century in many respects, with China a dominant economic power, trading partner, and military leader in the Asian continent. All of these aspects demonstrate that it is impossible to establish a nation as a competitive trading partner without also respecting its military, cultural, and social contribution to the world. This has been true for each world power in the past, and it will be true in the future as well.

China's economic history extends over many centuries. In fact, paper money originated in China. In A.D. 812, during the Tang Dynasty (618–907), a copper shortage made it impossible to mint coinage adequate for circulation demands; this led to the introduction of what came to be called flying money. (It was named this because a breeze could pick it up out of a person's hand and take it away, but the actual Chinese word for paper money was *kasu.*) No one at the time could have anticipated how popular paper money would become. Within 150 years, Chinese paper money had become the dominant medium of exchange, although the system was not fiat money at the time. Paper currency could be traded on demand for coins, salt, or tea. Fiat money has value based on the issuing government's declaration (or fiat). Legal tender consisting of coins has intrinsic value based on the rarity of the metal used (copper, zinc, silver, gold). The danger of the fiat monetary system—as history has shown— is that its use leads to inflation. In the United States, a fiat system (Federal Reserve notes) has been in use since the 1970s. At the time of China's experiment with paper money—which was not a fiat system because value was directly tied to commodities—the rest of the world had never heard of such an idea.

In the thirteenth century, Marco Polo took some samples of paper money with him and returned to Europe, where his explanations about the use of paper money were not believed. He wrote at the time:

> All these pieces of paper are issued with as much solemnity and authority as if they were pure gold or silver; and on every piece a variety of officials, whose duty it is, have to write their names, and to put their seals. And when all is duly prepared, the chief officer deputed by the Khan smears the Seal entrusted to him with vermilion, and impresses it on the paper, so that the form of the Seal remains printed upon it in red; the Money is then authentic.[2]

The convenience of paper money over metal coins made paper currency a practical medium in trade. The currency initially in use served as a draft or promissory note, but it was not considered official government currency until the eleventh century. During the Song Dynasty (907–960), paper currency was formalized and became government issued. In Szechuan province, banknotes were issued with pictures of people, trees, and buildings. The government took over control of paper money in the year 1023 and, for the first time, a specific value was established to monitor and regulate exchange between paper money and coinage.

During the Chin Dynasty (1115–1234) in north China, two kinds of paper money were in use. In 1154 the government established a Bureau of Paper Currency, which issued one bill of large denomination and a second bill worth fewer coins. In this experimental system, the issue of paper currency was limited to seven years; however, the Chin government did not back its currency with metal reserves and inflation became severe. The trend favoring paper money continued in popularity, however, with subsequent dynasties printing their own versions. During the Yuan Dynasty (1264–1368), excessive printing depreciated the value of paper money and, between 1260 and 1309, paper money depreciated by over 1,000 percent. Paper money eventually went west with the Mongols and came into use in the Middle East, where it also caused inflation. In 1601, the first European paper money was printed in Sweden.

The use of paper money in trade and commerce has maintained its popularity throughout modern history. However, everywhere that fiat money systems have been established, devaluation and inflation have soon followed.

Today, the use of fiat money is widespread. This is important to investors because the exchange rates of major industrialized nations are unavoidably tied together. When China's currency was pegged to the U.S. dollar, a number of other Asian currency policies did the same. Even though the Chinese currency was unpegged in mid-2005, it still closely follows the U.S. dollar. So in essence, as the U.S. dollar's fortunes go, so go the fortunes of Chinese currency, and, realistically, the currencies of other Asian nations would suffer along with China's should the U.S. dollar be devalued.

If nothing else, the monetary partnership between China and the United States makes it essential that the two countries work together. The economic requirements of each nation are tied to the continuation of current economic interests of the other. In the long run, this monetary situation will prove to work as a positive influence for both sides, preferable to a competitive position in which one side attempts to outtrade the other. Both countries—and investors on both sides of the Pacific—are coming to recognize the importance of working together as trading partners rather than as economic competitors.

THE UNITED STATES IN 1900

Considerable insight about the conditions in China today can be gained by reviewing where the United States was 100 years ago. In many respects, China is poised to explode economically in the near future, just as the United States was in 1900.

At the beginning of the twentieth century, few cars could be found in the United States and, of course, there were no road systems to speak of. No air travel was available, and the common means for short-term travel—the horse or horse and buggy—were limited in many ways. Long-term travel was achieved by train. The United States was primarily a rural country and the majority of its citizens lived in small towns, on farms, or in relatively small urban centers. Most people never traveled more than 20 or 30 miles from the place they were born. This is a difficult world to imagine today.

There is more. The concept of *retirement* was virtually unheard-of, and no such thing as a pension plan even existed. Life expectancy was about 40 years for males, and people generally worked until they died. In the investment markets, few people actually put money into stocks, and the whole mutual fund market didn't even exist. The first fund would not be developed until 1924.[3]

With all of the change that has occurred throughout the twentieth century, the world today looks vastly different. Even so, in looking for any recurring long-term themes in the changing world of investing, the thing that is striking is the lack of such themes. It appears that, rather than finding a consistent formula for identifying today's investment opportunities, the circumstances unique to a specific period dictate how investors can profit. And the preceding century's formula will not work today.

For example, the United States in the beginning of the twentieth century had already exhausted the infrastructure investment opportunities abundant only a few years before. The point to be made here is that, even when you identify a theme that works today as an investment opportunity, it is not necessarily safe to assume that the opportunity is permanent. Imagine how the world would change if cheap, efficient, safe energy sources were found tomorrow or next year. This would revolutionize not only the immediate energy sector, but entire national growth curves as well, not to mention the geopolitical ramifications. In China, one inhibiting factor to continuing expansion is the demand for energy. China is not able to meet all of its industrial energy demand, not to mention the simple residential requirement. As China grows, this problem will become more acute, so one of two things must happen: Either China and the rest of the industrialized world will need to find new and more efficient sources of energy or the *cost* of energy consumption will have to rise dramatically.

Among the initiatives to find better sources of energy are many new technologies for existing and known energy sources, such as coal and nuclear sources, and development of synthetic products from hydrogen and other possible sources. A growing percentage of energy requirements is derived from nuclear sources in China and elsewhere, and this trend will change in the near future as well, mandated by growing demand and by shrinking reserves of known energy sources such as oil.

Historically, investors have not anticipated short-term investment themes with consistency. In the nineteenth century, it seemed apparent that long-term investment growth would be achieved through railroad and canal development, but this observation did not anticipate the development of the automobile and airplane. Using an analogy of bowls of water that tilt and overflow, investment tendency is described based on a widespread gathering of facts from the financial media and then reacting, so that:

> investment themes only become obvious to most investors long after they have emerged—only once the bowl has been leaning and overflowing to one side for quite some time and created a bull market in a particular sector. Not surprisingly, we find that the largest flow of money into an asset class such as stocks, bonds, real estate or commodities will occur when just about everybody has fully understood the new theme—which will inevitably coincide with that sector's peak in popularity in prices. This has to be so, because once all the money has poured from the oversized bowl into one sector of the economy, that sector becomes grossly overpriced relative to sectors that haven't benefited from the torrential flows.[4]

This recurring dilemma—defining the need for a contrarian approach to investing at the very least—is typical not only of relatively small sectors within a domestic economy, but also in larger markets as well. Thus, a country's growth curve and investment bull market may enjoy and suffer its own cyclical trend just as market sectors do. The advice to buy low and sell high is cliché but remains wise, nonetheless, because so many people do the opposite.

When you look at the state of the United States in 1900, you quickly realize that it was as foreign a country as China is today to the U.S. investor. There is a tendency to proceed from the premise that "it has always been this way" in terms of how domestic stock markets work. However, you may have great difficulty imagining the pre-1924 world without mutual funds; the 1900 world without Social Security or, for that matter, any kind of retirement program; a world in which people's life expectancy was only 40 years; or a world without planes and automobiles. In such a world, it becomes apparent that the viewpoint of the investor of 1900 would be severely limited in comparison to today's investor.

Not only did the investor of 1900 have very little worldwide exposure; there was no Internet, limited telephone service, and virtually no instant communication overseas. In 1900, approximately 25 percent of the U.S. population had telephone service, under 20 million out of a population of 76 million people. Today, close to 100 percent of the United States has phone service (or has it available). In China today, a total of 532 million land line and cell phone customers are known to exist, together comprising about 40 percent of China's 1.3 billion population. (This is a liberal estimate, because it is likely that many people with phone service have both land line and cell phone accounts, so they are counted twice in these figures.)[5]

The parallel in levels of service reflects demographics in China today, as it did in the United States more than 100 years ago. China consists of distinct and starkly different regions, including a primarily agrarian northern area and industrialized, urban southern and coastal areas. Advanced technology is more likely to be found in densely populated urban areas, and less so in the more rural north. This was also the case in the United States from the telephone's invention in 1876 until 1900. During that period, the telephone was viewed in many sectors as a novelty or even as a nuisance. Katy Leary, housekeeper for famous American author Mark Twain, described Twain's disgust with the telephone:

> Shortly after the telephone invention . . . I went to Hartford. They had just put it in about that time and it made Mr. Clemens mad, "just to hear the damned thing ring," he said. Yes, that telephone used to make Mr. Clemens wild, because he would hear all right but he couldn't give his message out good. It wasn't very good service those days, and he used to fight the telephone girls all the time. He'd say, "Are you all asleep down there? If you don't give me better service you can

send somebody right up here and pull this thing out. I won't have this old thing in the house, it's a nuisance!"[6]

In the year 1900, an investor or would-be investor would be likely to seek opportunities based on what was then visible. This precludes the potential for mass-produced automobiles and trucks, air travel, and other inventions of the twentieth century—including computers and the Internet. The dominant mode of affordable communication in 1900 remained the telegraph, with the telephone moving quickly up in rank. However, an investor would not be able to see the future, and it is unlikely that predictions were being made about the impact of new inventions. An anecdote about the impossibility of predicting the future is found in the recurrent story of the head of the U.S. Patent Office tendering his resignation in 1845 on the basis that there was nothing left to invent. The story is not true; but anecdotally, it makes the point that at any given time, it is impossible to imagine what the future holds. The origin of the legend is found in a statement made in 1843 in a report to Congress, in which the commissioner of the Patent Office, Henry L. Ellsworth, included the following comment:

> "The advancement of the arts, from year to year, taxes our credulity and seems to presage the arrival of that period when human improvement must end." . . . When Commissioner Ellsworth did resign in 1845, his letter of resignation certainly gave no indication that he was resigning because he thought there was nothing left for the Patent Office to do. He gave as his reason the pressure of private affairs, and stated, "I wish to express a willingness that others may share public favors and have an opportunity to make greater improvements."[7]

A review of the events and technology that caused U.S. growth in the nineteenth century provides *some* insight into what is happening in China today. This does not necessarily mean that the same factors will be in play. However, it provides some interesting parallels in the way that we need to approach the identification of bull markets, investing opportunities, the course of world events, and the extent to which these may affect your investment timing and decisions.

EVENTS THAT FUELED NINETEENTH-CENTURY GROWTH IN THE UNITED STATES

Events during the Jacksonian era of the 1840s in the United States were characterized by the concept of Manifest Destiny, the idea that the United States had not only a mission but a right to expand westward and create a two-ocean continental nation. The country's population was growing, and several sources of pressure promoted the cause of Manifest Destiny. These included a high birth rate, augmented by growing rates of immigration. Immigration was encouraged because work was plentiful and foreign immigrants were seen as a source of cheap labor. Between 1800 and 1840, the U.S. population grew from five million to 23 million. Second, the dream of holding influence on two oceans was viewed by politicians as the means for turning the United States into a world power.

The expansion westward was no simple matter; it required tremendous investment in the nation's infrastructure. In the pre-automobile and pre-aviation era, this meant two primary methods of transportation: railroads and canals. In the midnineteenth century, people migrated in covered wagons, a romantic idea that in actuality was dangerous, difficult, and a lengthy trip. It is worth remembering that the United States is not far removed from covered wagon days; progress has been rapid. We may expect the same scale of explosive growth in China, in many ways.

In the case of U.S. growth, there were many notable differences in the way that migration occurred for families (such as wagon trains or an even longer trip around South America) versus expansion of commercial interests, which occurred by way of rail lines and canal development. It was clear to the political leaders of the day that expansion included military as well as geographic, economic, and cultural elements. During a series of administrations, presidents were able to acquire land from France, Spain, Mexico, and England, either by negotiation or through war. When it came to sustaining an economic vitality for a continental nation, it would also be necessary to create and maintain lines of transport and communication. Thus, raw materials and supplies would have to be moved from east to west efficiently and affordably; and a sustained expansion would require a careful coordination between land- and sea-based military power as well as economic supply lines.

The economic changes the United States experienced between 1840 and 1900 were significant in many ways. The United States established itself not only as a world military power but also as a successful trading partner for all parts of the globe.

Because the same level of significant shift is occurring today in China, an analysis of nineteenth-century America is instructive. The big difference now is that everything—communication, economic expansion, and world trade—occurs at a far more rapid pace than it did in the nineteenth century.

The Erie Canal represented an early but very significant part of the expansion in commercial interests. Completed in 1825, the 364-mile canal reduced travel time by 90 percent between New York and other cities such as Buffalo, Detroit, and Cleveland. The Great Lakes were subsequently connected to the St. Lawrence River via the Welland Canal, a second major connector from mid-America to the Atlantic Ocean. The canal boom made New York the most important commercial center of the United States, replacing Philadelphia in both population and import levels.

Just as speculation in the 1990s took place in Internet stocks, a similar pattern was seen in the canal boom of the 1820s and 1830s. Prices rose as promising new canal projects were proposed. An idea for an Illinois-Michigan Canal prompted wild speculation, both in construction stocks and in Chicago real estate. The canal would have connected Chicago's Lake Michigan port area to the Illinois River, thus to the Mississippi River and to St. Louis. Stock prices collapsed in 1837, however, and Chicago land values plummeted 90 percent. When the canal was finally completed, it made Chicago a major port and improved its commercial value; but most investors and land speculators had gone broke in the process. This is instructive. The economic lesson of history reveals that *demand* may ensure the success of economic and infrastructure projects, but it does not ensure that investors will profit from the change.

Between the high bank, trust, and railroad stock prices of 1837 and the bust in 1841, fortunes were lost. Figure 2.1 shows how the numbers changed in only four years.

This illustration indicates that the bust in Internet stocks was not the first such instance of rapid profitability within a single (or new) market sector. These types of boom-and-bust periods have occurred predictably throughout market history; and they will occur again in the future. As China continues investing in mining, energy, and transportation infrastructure, the applicable corporate sectors (both private and state owned) will rise in value, go through cyclical change, and eventually fall. However, profits must be timed carefully, as history also demonstrates that nothing—not even permanent infrastructure investment—remains profitable forever.

Considering the vast number of railroads in existence in the United States in the nineteenth century and the few remaining today, it is doubtful that any long-term investments in rail transport would have been profitable without end. The same is true for companies

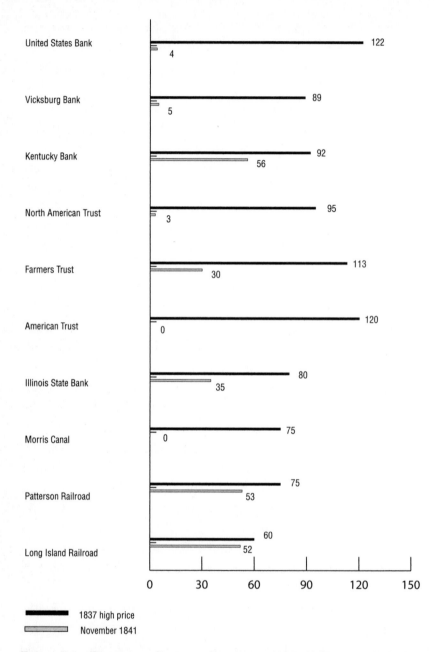

FIGURE 2.1   DECLINE OF SELECTED COMPANIES 1837–1841
Source: Robert Sobel, *Panic on Wall Street* (New York: Truman Talley Books/Dutton, 1988; new ed., Frederick, MD: Beard Books, 1999).

investing in canals. In the case of Illinois, by 1841 the state itself went into default. Numerous banks and railroads suffered equally as prices collapsed, not to mention Chicago real estate prices.

The canal speculation was not limited to U.S. companies. A lesson can be learned about overseas investing by looking at the example of the Bank of England. In 1836, English gold reserves were cut in half as money flowed into speculative ventures in the booming U.S. economy. The bank was forced to lower its rediscount rate twice, leading to economic panic and the closure of several English banks. By 1837, interest rates in England had risen to 15 percent. This also created a sudden cutoff of investment capital from England to the United States, which had a secondary effect. Besides the concerns summarized in the chart, in the two years from 1837 to 1839 at least 1,500 U.S. banks also failed.

A parallel to more recent events makes the point that international trends are interconnected. Just as English investment dried up and broke many U.S. banks, the Asian crisis of 1997 was caused by a similar effect—foreign investors' unwillingness to finance rising current account deficits in Asian countries. The unparalleled enthusiasm in England for investments in U.S. expansion failed to anticipate the problems that soon came up. By the same token, publications watching Asian trends also failed to see what was soon to come. By 1995, glowing predictions had been offered up for years in magazines like the *Far Eastern Economic Review*, in which the prediction was made about Asia's future:

> What is happening in Asia is by far the most important development in the world. Nothing else comes close, not only for Asians but the entire planet. The modernization of Asia will forever reshape the world as we move toward the next millennium. In the 1990s Asia came of age. As we move toward the year 2000, Asia will become the dominant region in the world; economically, politically and culturally. We are on the threshold of the Asian Renaissance.[8]

This and similar optimistic predictions did not predict the looming crisis, nor did they read any of the signs leading up to 1997. Asian stocks had begun to weaken by 1995. Both Thai and Indian currencies fell disastrously against the dollar and, unlike other economic crises (like Mexico in 1995), it did not end suddenly. It was prolonged, in fact, particularly because so many foreign investors were involved in having financed expanded current account deficits in Asian economies. The resulting lowering in confidence (and expectations) only extended the crisis. A major difference between the nineteenth-century United States situation and the one in Asia in 1997 was in emphasis. The United States crisis involved investment in expansion—railroads and canals—in a primarily agrarian economy. The severity of the losses in the 1840s was made worse by a softening in demand in the cotton market, which was a mainstay of the United States economy of the era. In modern-day Asia, a more diversified economy involves a broad range of technology and manufacturing, but little in the way of farm products and prices. The currency exchange problems faced by numerous Asian countries in the 1997 crisis may be an equivalent of English and United States bank failures 150 years earlier, but today's economy—and the cyclical downturn likely to occur within it—involves natural resources more than agricultural products, trade deficits adding to external debt, international labor market movements and labor cost competition, actual movement of money rather than overseas investment (often in the form of lending and investment in foreign debt securities), and the immediate effects of currency exchange between international fiat currency systems.

Many predictions are made concerning the coming new age in China. A decade ago, all of Asia was seen as the so-called new economy, but after the 1997 collapse, China has become clearly the center of this thought, with India in second place. This has been a subtle shift, but an important one. As is always the case, predictions were overly broad, and have been focused based on more recent events. But can growth occur without pause? Are any temporary setbacks possible (or even likely) in China's ascent to the position of dominant economic power? It is almost certain that there will be some bumps on the road. However, the probable course of China's growth curve involves economic strength and continuing dominance in many sectors.

PREDICTION: EVENTS FUELING CHINA'S GROWTH IN THE TWENTY-FIRST CENTURY

Clearly, China is on a path of expansion; there is no mistaking that. The question remains, however: What specific factors (thus, market sectors) will lead this growth?

Overall, China's economic output is anticipated to triple by the year 2020 from 2005 levels, and to surpass the output of the United States and Japan by midcentury. A part of this broad economic trend involves improving the standard of living of Chinese citizens. Since 1980, 300 million people have been lifted out of poverty as the average person's income has grown by 400 percent.[9] Even so, the problem persists as well as the obvious disparity between the urban south and coast versus the agrarian northern areas of China. These disparities are not merely economic; they cause resentments between population and demographic groups, augmenting the already apparent inconsistencies between regions. Even so, we can judge the severity of these differences best in economic terms. For example, urban per capita GDP is higher than $3,000 in United States dollars, whereas the average farmer's GDP level is at 30 percent of those levels, or about $900 per year.[10]

These recent impressive numbers reveal a fast-paced change in China's domestic economy. But can it be sustained? And to the extent that growth will continue, how and where will it occur? These are the essential questions that investors outside of China need to pin down in order to know specifically where and how to invest. It is no easy task, because China is not a single entity, defined by a single set of demographic or economic circumstances. In fact, China is undergoing transformation on several levels because the country consists of dissimilar geographic interests and demographic characteristics.

Most countries undergoing transition can be defined by a singular set of factors, and those factors affect the entire population. However, China has two major transitional challenges. First, its previously agrarian economy is being moved gradually into a modern and industrialized economy. Second, its twentieth-century planned economy is rapidly being transformed into a market economy. The duality of this process is particularly challenging, not only to the government of China, but also to the people. A natural rivalry for resources, reform, and institutional change take time and cannot occur at the same speed everywhere. In many respects, part of China has remained feudal in character, while another part has become rapidly industrialized.

Reasonably, anyone observing China recognizes that a big part of the reform needed is going to involve elimination or reform of state-owned enterprises (SOEs). The inefficiency of the SOE sector—which remains a substantial portion of the economy—has been an inhibiting factor and has even added to social discord in some provinces. Unemployment levels among state employees are a chronic problem, and in the banking sector, the levels of nonperforming loans (NPLs) have caused deflation and affect overall banking profits. The numbers tell the story in economic terms. The nonstate sector (privately owned concerns, the self-employed, publicly traded companies, and international joint ventures) accounted by 2002 for 74 percent of industrial output, 62 percent of GDP, and 100 percent of employment growth not including the offsetting of unemployment in SOEs).[11]

The trend away from SOEs and toward a market economy involves three major subtrends. These are:

1. Increasing competitive success in the nonstate market sector as demonstrated by the numbers.

2. Growth in nonstate sector jobs, a major ongoing shift in which 15 million state employees lost jobs in five years between 1997 and 2002 without causing instability due to this job shift.

3. Rapid increases in private capital investment.

Within this trend, which may also be largely called a type of privatization, massive social change is occurring. This largest population in the world is gradually undergoing an economic revolution of unprecedented scale, and much of that has been invisible. For example, in some regions an estimated 70 percent of smaller SOEs have been quietly privatized in one way or another—sold to employees in a style akin to United States–type employee stock ownership plan (ESOP) programs of the past, and converted into employee-owned share-based companies.[12]

The relatively subtle shift away from SOEs to private enterprise or publicly listed companies is only one aspect of this dual transformation. The social and cultural changes that accompany this change may be more significant in the long run. Income disparity among various demographic segments in China may cause not only growth pangs but social unrest as well. In a sense, this problem was created in the past, when the socialist regime imposed an overequalized society. The relatively new market system with its market-driven competitive forces and profit incentives is characterized by ever-growing disparity in income levels. Also, the many social improvements, such as removal of large portions of the population from poverty, are *average* outcomes but do not apply everywhere within China. The largely rural north has experienced less growth and less positive change than the industrialized, urbanized south, for example. It is not only a rural-versus-urban problem. Laid-off employees of previous SOEs who are now 40 or older are having difficulty getting retraining and finding jobs in a competitive job market. The lack of extensive retraining programs means that, even with the overall improvements in income levels among the population, some demographic segments may fall between the cracks in Chinese society. This occurs in all economic transitions; it is never accurate to assume that recognizable change is universal across all demographic segments of a society. The differences in China are more complex, though, because of the complexities of geographic, demographic, and economic differences within the country. In this respect, it is inaccurate to think of China as a singular country (economically speaking) because so many different forces of change are at work.

These disparities, notably in regional terms, are sensitive social and political issues. These problems, though, are not dividing China; in fact, market forces do have universal benefit, and China is probably more united today than ever before. The problem is that the rate of improvement is not identical everywhere. It is to be expected that northern rural populations are going to be resentful of the more rapid improvement in lifestyle and standard of living in the southern and coastal areas, where urban and industrial growth is much more rapid. The changes in per capita income among different regions are not caused solely by emphasis on industrial growth; neither are the disparities all moving in the same direction. In fact, in some respects, the trends are beginning to shift favorably.

As the coastal and southern living standards and wages improve, investment has begun moving inland along the Yangtze River. In regions such as Anhui and Hubei, growth has exceeded coastal growth rates since 1998. Internal immigration affects the overall picture, too. Also since 1998, over 20 million citizens have migrated out of the rural north to southern and coastal areas, seeking improved lifestyles and better wages.

INHIBITING FACTORS TO ECONOMIC GROWTH

The trends in China are promising; in fact, even the disparity between rural and urban populations is not entirely negative. The growth levels may vary, but it is an overall positive cultural and economic sign. Economic growth never moves upward in a straight line, either. Many factors may inhibit or slow down the growth curve.

When investors seek growth prospects or bull markets, they tend to believe that growth is going to occur in an unending straight line. This is hardly ever the case. China is a situation in which any number of inhibiting factors may arise, and it is smart to be aware of these as part of an overall analysis of investment potential. The problems include nonperforming loans (NPLs), unemployment, income disparities by region, unchanged rural poverty, and corruption.

The previously mentioned nonperforming loans have been and remain a major inhibitor to sustained growth. Until mid-2005, the Chinese state banking system officially pegged the rate of NPLs at approximately 25 percent of GDP. However, the actual rate including NPLs transferred into asset management groups may be as high as 40 percent of GDP, with a major factor being problems associated with SOEs.[13] A part of this trend has been a gradual shift of fiscal responsibility away from SOEs and toward state banks. Essentially, given the transitional nature of China's economy today, these NPLs are less like western-style loan defaults and more like government deficits. It is difficult to make a comparison, for example, between Chinese and United States loan trends, because of the involvement of the Chinese government in the financial sector of the past.

A similar problem occurs when an attempt is made to equate Chinese unemployment with the same trend in the United States. In the complexities of the Chinese economy, the separate varieties of unemployment, each with its own significance in the larger economic trend, make familiar comparisons difficult and even impossible. In the United States, unemployment is subdivided by sectors, but the tendency is to view unemployment as a single nationwide economic factor. China, in comparison, contends with three distinct problems: urban unemployment, which has averaged approximately 3.5 percent; rural unemployment and underemployment, which is more difficult to define because the rural population is generally underemployed; and unemployed former state workers, who after reform find themselves out of work contrary to the previous socialist social contract promising work to everyone.

Associated with urban unemployment is an odd quirk: a large number of migrated farm workers who are undertrained and seeking work, versus unfilled demand for skilled work and a shortage of trained personnel. The underemployment of rural workers grows from the fact that about three-quarters of rural families own land, but many of those plots are so small that those families are not as self-sustaining as a fully employed worker would be. (In this regard, a comparison between Chinese rural underemployment and western-style rural unemployment is very difficult to make.) The third group, ex–state workers, poses a special problem for the government. From 1997 through 2001, 24 million state workers lost their jobs, and their status is a drain on the state welfare system. These workers receive minimum payments that are higher than unemployment as well as some limited retraining. However, it will take many years to absorb these 24 million people into the economy.

No relief should be expected from the ever-shrinking SOE sector. Many SOEs are having their own financial problems and, aside from not hiring any new workers, often are unable to pay those already on their payrolls. Some workers' wages may be delayed up to 10 months. Job trends show that the nonstate sector is creating new jobs, complete with better wage levels. Those SOE employees who have lost their jobs compete with nonstate sector workers. The Chinese government has increased payments to its relocation effort through the Urban Reemployment Center (URC).[14] Unfortunately, the problem is massive, and improvements will take many years to be completed.

Income disparities by region continue to be a problem for China and may inhibit growth well into the future. The situation is improving, albeit gradually. This is as much a political issue as an economic one. Slow growth in rural areas is not caused solely by industrialization in coastal and southern areas. There has also been a concentration of SOEs in the north; thus, solving the problem will have to involve not only changes in the standard of living of rural families but actual reform of the SOE system over time.

Closely related to the income disparity is the unchanged rural poverty in the northern regions. The large-scale migration away from rural and into urban areas creates problems of its own in terms of employment and training, congestion, and ongoing poverty. The transition away from the rural emphasis of the past is a long-term and slow-moving transition for China, in which only about 15 percent of the total land is arable. Over half of the population is employed in this rural economy, but it contributes only a small portion of total GDP. The problems of feeding a growing urban population from a chronically poor rural area, in which incentives continue for younger people to abandon the traditional life and move to the big cities, may be a major future inhibiting factor to continued growth, not to mention the challenges of training people on a massive scale to fill the demand for jobs.

The last problem inhibiting growth—corruption—is also gradually changing in China. In the past, it has proven to be a large problem, but since 1998 many reforms have gone into effect and the problem is shrinking. This does not mean it will disappear entirely, and it may add to future problems in economic terms. The problem is closely associated with SOEs, and this is explained as having everything to do with corruption itself:

> A great part of the problem of corruption is tied to the existence of big state-owned economic sectors, not only the government bureaucracy and political structure. Therefore, the privatization of the SOEs and reforms of other state-owned institutions will be one of the key factors in reducing corruption.[15]

Another potential inhibiting factor to continued economic growth is demographic. To most people, this means population trends, the simple number of people within a country. In the case of China, the question is far more complex. The potential problem is associated not only with how many mouths must be fed and families housed, but also with *where* those people live. The migration away from the rural areas and into the cities has both a positive and a negative impact. To the extent that new workers fill demand while holding labor costs down, the migration improves overall GDP and reduces national poverty. However, the trend may also increase unemployment among untrained workers, not to mention creating housing shortages, congestion, and crowding in the urban regions.

Associated with the population trend is the employment trend. The fact that untrained worker unemployment is offset by unfilled skilled jobs underscores the importance of the need for sweeping changes in training programs. In order to compete globally, China will need to improve its training of skilled workers. There is no shortage of low-wage factory and manufacturing employees; but what China will need for future growth will be higher-paid, well-trained skilled employees, notably in technology and technological manufacturing industries.

Another potential problem limiting unbridled growth is already being experienced in China, as demonstrated in the last chapter.

Finally, China will continue to compete on the international level. Its numerous domestic problems are ongoing and have to be overcome gradually, involving investment, cultural change, management of a migrating population, and improving the lifestyle of its citizens. At the same time, China needs to remain competitive on an international level. No nation is self-sufficient in the twenty-first century, and China depends on its trading partners on many, many levels. It must import energy resources, raw materials, and expertise in many industries. The country also has to manage a considerable financial threat involving both its own currency and those currencies of its trading partners. This international aspect to China's domestic growth challenge is explored in the next chapter.

CHAPTER 3

ECONOMIC FORCES AT WORK

T HE WHOLE transition of China as it evolves into an economic power is a major and, in some respects, an impossible to comprehend phenomenon today. Just as the impact of the Asian and European black plagues, the Age of Discovery, the Industrial Revolution, the telephone, computer, Internet, and other significant events and discoveries took the world by surprise, the same is true with China's new free-market world strategy. As an investor outside of China and looking in, you cannot possibly anticipate all the successes (or failures) of the future. Neither can you know with certainty exactly how this change will affect you. One thing is certain: From this point forward, the population of the free-market economy is in the process of growing by billions.

And exactly what does this mean? How can you profit from this massive shift in emphasis, power, and potential? Investors can either follow what everyone else is doing or they can seek out emerging trends and opportunities. Followers may earn profits, but those who are able to look ahead are more likely to earn big profits. The challenge is going to be in identifying specific opportunities, and in thinking beyond what may seem obvious. For example, investors usually assume that by identifying a specific demand, it is only necessary to identify companies situated to meet that demand, and that is an investment opportunity of the future. In terms of investing in China, this formula might not work.

Chinese investment prospects are complicated by the existence of SOEs and their part in the Chinese economy; the multi-level growth and expansion of the Chinese economy (not only in manufacturing of consumer products, but also in electronics and technology); increased research and development (R&D) investment from outside of China; problems associated with meeting demand for skilled employees; and chronic energy demands. On top of this, internal demographic migration is vast, and the poverty level among rural populations continues to lag behind the urban trend. Even so, investors have an advantage in China because the real growth is yet to come.

To achieve this advantage, you have to be able to adopt an objective view of markets, where they have been, and where trends are moving. To do this, it helps to make comparisons to similar situations in the past, or to be able to look at issues from a broad perspective. For example, you know that China is the world's largest coal producer, but the country imports coal. Why? It is cheaper to buy coal and import it than it is to mine and transport coal from the far northern regions to the industrial south. This oddity points out not only a problem, but an opportunity as well: Once China develops technology to produce liquid coal, construct pipelines, and move the resource to the industrial areas, the problem will be solved. In fact, many similar problems will be solved, and such solutions are to be expected during a period of massive national transition. The chronic power shortage will disappear, dependence on Middle East oil will diminish, power-related inhibitions to extended growth will be removed, and China's industrial-area environmental conditions will be improved. All of these outcomes are promising indicators for investment in those companies working on the coal technology (as well as similar trends involving nuclear, hydrogen, and other alternative energy resources). Furthermore, it removes potential growth inhibitors from energy-dependent industries, so investors concerned about long-term prospects in

China's industrial sector would be reassured by these developments, assuming that it is possible to identify the likely timing of these developments.

It is not that difficult, either. If you look ahead to the *known* timing when China and the rest of the world will reach saturation given current supply and current usage of oil, the development of alternative technologies becomes urgent. History has shown that when necessity forces the issue, new technology comes to pass. If such changes and shifts do not occur, then neither will growth.

This type of analysis is not limited to the question of where to invest capital; it also indicates where *not* to invest. For example, oil exploration and development, oil equipment, and even oil and gas refining are powerful and important industries today. However, what will happen to these companies if and when emphasis shifts away from oil? Will these corporations make the shift and maintain their position or will they become obsolete? Given the need for new energy technology, the sure thing of today's oil industry looks far more uncertain in the future.

Meanwhile, China is becoming increasingly dependent on Middle East oil, even as new technologies are being developed. Even with its rapid increase in nuclear power plants, hydroelectric facilities, and research into other technologies, China's oil imports increase each year. By 2010, the country will need a minimum of 120 million tons of oil imports per year, and more in years beyond. This strains not only world supplies and prices of oil, but forces China to compete with other oil-dependent nations, notably the United States.[1]

The changes under way in China are complex. This complicates the investment decisions everyone needs to make in the future as well as today. You need to analyze developments based on today's supply and demand, future technological changes, global as well as country-specific trends, and the likely cyclical changes in both infrastructure and investment markets.

A GOLIATH WITH MANY HEADS

If you keep in mind the fact that China is *not* a single economy, it will be easier to understand how the country's economy and capital strategies work. Because China is vast and has many separate demographic and economic groups, we need to comprehend an area or region rather than a consistently governed, singular entity.

In the United States, investors are accustomed to one set of rules, one regulatory environment, and one cultural attitude about the economy and investing. There exists a degree of political conflict, naturally. The political left is resentful toward the rich who they feel don't pay their fair share of taxes and the right-wing administration that they feel changes tax laws to help the administration's wealthy friends. The far right resents the welfare mentality of the left and the entitlement state that has been created and added to since the New Deal of the 1930s. However, when all is said and done, politics and economics don't mix well, and with respect to the process of investing and making money, U.S. citizens are of the same mind. Not so in China.

The complexity of the social, political, and economic system in China is mind-boggling. Economically, China's growth, if anything, is occurring too rapidly. The question of whether China's financial system can keep up is worthy of consideration. (More on this later in this chapter.) When you review fixed capital spending in China, you discover that it comes out to 43 percent of the nation's GDP, the seventh-largest in the world, and that is too high a level to sustain. By comparison, the United States came in at number 122 out of 145 nations, so China's spending levels are both high and *relatively* high, an important distinction.[2]

The dollar value is equal to approximately U.S. $600 billion per year invested in capital projects. You may appreciate the significance of such capital infrastructure investment by again thinking about the United States during the nineteenth century and its westward expansion. It is a similar phenomenon in China today. However, China is not spending money on railroads, dams, and nuclear power plants alone. That is only a part of the bigger picture. In fact, about one-fourth of total annual capital spending is in manufacturing. Interestingly, no one category within the larger manufacturing sector accounts for more than 3.5 percent of the total—a signal that China's controlled manufacturing expansion is broad or, as investors would describe it, diversified.[3]

Investors can learn a lot about potential growth—both in terms of industry itself and potential for equity investments—by reviewing where this growth is taking place. Investment in fixed assets is only one indicator, though. Investors should also look at growth rates overall, that is to say, expansion in terms of industry size and rate of change.

It's no surprise that a lot of expansion is taking place in the energy sector. The primary energy subsectors (oil processing, coking plants, and nuclear) are growing at a rate of 127 percent, using 2003 numbers. The energy demand comes not solely from residential use, but more so from other manufacturing industries. Wood processing, furniture manufacturing, and metal product industries all expanded by over 50 percent in the latest reporting year.[4]

From the investment point of view, all industry depends on availability of energy. So the energy sector is a major growth industry of its own, just from sheer necessity. Investors should certainly keep an eye on China's energy markets, but to the extent that expansion continues within energy, it will affect every other Chinese manufacturing segment as well. Without more energy, expansion will come to a grinding halt. Continuing on the current course, that would be inevitable. Therefore, either China will be at the forefront of innovative new energy technology or growth itself will not last.

Returning to the comparison between twenty-first-century China and nineteenth-century America, how is infrastructure investment moving along? In the United States, the railroad and canal era was defined by massive investment by both government and U.S.-based corporations, as well as an unhealthy level of outright speculation. This was augmented by substantial debt capitalization from both U.S.-based banks and foreign banks, notably in England. In fact, the nineteenth century was marked by a series of crises in banking as optimistic speculation dominated Chicago's real estate, canal markets, banks lending for capital expansion, railroads, and, in general, financing for just about any expansion plan. Following the 1848 canal construction craze, the United States went through a brief period of railroad building during the 1850s. Strong economic signals encouraged investment in these infrastructure projects, on the assumption that strong demand for goods supported the obvious need for more miles of rail. Even though this is generally logical, it is not unlimited; at some point, any cyclical trend stops and then turns, and in the case of both canal and railroad expansion, speculators and lenders alike ignored the cyclical nature of the booming economy. In 1857 inflation and weakening economic signals changed everything. A lot of the growth had been generated by the big gold discovery in California the decade before. Railroad expansion enabled growth in many industries such as pig iron, coal production, and mining in general. Both mining stocks and railroad stocks were popular, even among investors who had lost money in the canal craze a decade earlier and had decided to never speculate in U.S. ventures again. However, like all economic trends, the economic cycle of the 1850s eventually ran out of steam.

Ignoring the signals in a long-standing and universal tradition of investors and speculators, both domestic and foreign money flocked to railroad shares. The railroad index, however, had peaked by 1852 and European liquidity had been drained by the Crimean War (1854–1856) just at the point that the railroad investment industry was accelerating. The result—too many securities and not enough capital—remained a chronic problem until 1857 even though many economic conditions, such as consumer demand, remained strong.

The point to be made here concerning China is that economic forces do not always determine viability of a particular investment. In the case of railroad stocks in the United States in the nineteenth century, several factors—strong economic indicators, a discovery of gold, and aggressive westward expansion—did not help this market because foreign investors did not have capital available to keep up with the rate of expansion. Furthermore, the strength of an economy in general does not always mean that a particular sector is going to continue to grow, even when it is feeding such demand. The underlying economic situation has to be monitored closely for a peak in activity, outside activity, levels of liquidity among the sources of equity (and debt) funding, and more.

The same disparity between economics and markets could easily occur in China. Events in areas outside of China could easily affect the investment markets. A lot of emphasis and worry among analysts is focused on internal strife (poverty, demographic conflicts, migration, energy shortages), but it is equally possible that uncontrollable events outside of China will affect the rate of expansion just as much. A shortage of Middle East oil, heating up in the war on terrorism, a major outbreak of a pandemic, catastrophic earthquakes and tsunamis—these are only a few of the possible events that could affect momentum in China's economic expansion, even though none of these are actual economic forces in and of themselves.

Market conditions will also affect investment values. There is a tendency to think that market forces—supply and demand—are the sole indicators defining profitable investments. However, this is not the case. Looking again to history, the cause of the U.S. financial crisis of the 1850s had several components, but it occurred in a period in which economic indicators were quite strong. The cause of the late-decade crisis, more than any other, was excessive speculation. Therefore, the most remote of events, such as a drain of European liquidity due to a distant war, sparked the financial crisis without any direct influence from economic indicators. The same factors could come into play in China, not to mention an internal currency crisis. With the Chinese currency closely aligned to the U.S. dollar, a devaluation in the United States would immediately affect the entire Chinese economy. Furthermore, inconsistency in accounting standards in different Chinese markets may cause chaos both at home and among international capital sources. Until the accounting inconsistency is cleaned up, overseas doubts will remain. This, like so many aspects in China's market transition, may require years to reform.

Investors looking to China during its current and future era of expansion should keep these realities in mind. This historical viewpoint is not limited to the United States. Following the period between 1866 and 1873, expansion in Europe—especially in Germany, Austria, and Prussia—following the Franco-Prussian War was rapid and characterized again by accelerated market speculation. In this time frame, new companies were being formed in Prussia at a spectacular rate, and speculators saw no end in sight. An author of the period described conditions, which sound oddly like the dot-com craze of recent years, followed by the U.S. mortgage bubble:

> The real object of banks and companies was quite lost sight of, and men were swept into the whirl of speculation without having any other desire than to gamble and to make money in the lottery of the share market . . . building speculations were indeed among the most unsound and ruinous of all the business of the time. The price of land was run up to a purely fictitious level, and loans were made to cover the sites with houses to an extent which, when the crash came, rendered it impossible to recover even a fraction of the principal.[5]

The familiar ring to this description applies not only to nineteenth-century U.S. speculation, to Europe in the 1870s, or to the United States during the Internet stock era; it also applies to future speculative activity in potentially a broad range of Chinese market sectors. Whether viewed economically or from a market point of view, investors need to move ahead cautiously, recognizing the fact that markets in China are unique; the rules vary by region; and internal accounting standards are not consistent, with possibly one of three or more different reporting standards in play.

Even looking back to recent activity in China, you can learn a lot about investment potential (and risk) in developing situations. A valid comparison may be drawn between U.S. railroad and canal shares of the nineteenth century and Chinese infrastructure, transportation, mining, and telephone stocks of the 1990s. The unbridled optimism of the 1990s era concerning investment potential throughout Southeast Asia is rarely mentioned today, but it did lead to speculation and, in many sectors, to big losses. In a sense, smart investing in China in the twenty-first century requires a new approach, a sort of international contrarianism. Why? Remember, overseas opportunities do not present themselves simply because domestic markets are in a downturn. There is a tendency to look overseas when domestic economic trends are weak. To some extent, weak economic trends in one place can show up opportunities elsewhere. However, it is a mistake to move money overseas primarily because of weak conditions at home. Increasingly, a global cause and effect makes this strategy questionable; domestic indicators may, in fact, by symptomatic of a global economic cycle.

This is particularly true if you invest in infrastructure based on apparent economic signs. The two may not go together as you may wish. For example, increased demand for energy does not always mean that shares of hydroelectric development companies are going to rise in value. Investing in infrastructure projects via stock of companies whose activities are related to those developments is not always going to be profitable, at least not in the expected time frame. Such outcomes often are more the result of international speculation than of any fundamental indicators, capital strength of corporations, or quality of management. You may need to look more closely at what market sentiment reveals than at the company's financial condition, market position, and activity.

In the United States, investors have seen, time and again, well-positioned corporations, in the middle of evolving technologies, that have failed to deliver growth to investors. The causes are varied and or complex: failure to capitalize on emerging markets, poor management, or competition, for example. The same problems should be expected to occur in Chinese markets as the economic transition continues. No changing economy moves smoothly or universally, and investors in any new market should proceed with enthusiasm, tempered with caution.

THE ENERGY EQUATION IN CHINA

The problem for investors is making a connection between market demand and investment profits. It would seem logical that the two would work in conjunction, and that, where demand exists, sound investment opportunities would abound. However, that is not always the case.

The energy crisis in China is connected directly to the ever-expanding infrastructure investment by the Chinese government, by expanding industry, and by competitive forces. The speed of development underscores this problem as well. In recent years, transportation investment was 11.5 percent of all fixed asset spending, road construction was 7.6 percent, and water projects were 8.2 percent. Together, this is over one-fourth of the total, representing incredible energy and infrastructure requirements, with more to come.[6]

The comparisons to other countries are interesting and they reveal where all of this investment is going. Expanding facilities relating to increased industrial output and production of energy facilitates future growth. Even if demand were to fall off for manufactured goods, it is cyclical and tends to return. In the United States, very little is being invested in manufacturing of tangible goods. In fact, 60 percent of business investment in the United States is spent on computer software and hardware. The United States is holding onto its dominance in information technology (IT), but it has to keep spending because IT goes obsolete very rapidly. Not so with factories.

The comparison doesn't end there. New factories and expanded industries create new jobs, whereas expanded IT investment does not, at least not at the same levels. So on the broad economic picture, China's economic expansion competes against U.S. IT dominance and, ultimately, the manufacturing sector is more likely to win the race. It becomes a race, in fact, between investment in technologies with a small job base and relatively high salary requirements and investment in manufacturing with a large employment base and lower wages.

Considering the impact of expansion of factories and accelerated rates of manufactured goods, the ever-growing energy requirements become critical at some point. China is already consuming a huge portion of world resources and estimates are that the coastal areas of the country could see growth of up to 20 new cities in the next two decades, each with populations between 15 million and 30 million people.[7] The more population migration China experiences, the more jobs it will need to create in industrial areas and the more resources it will need to consume.

Economists tend to think about expanded productivity in terms of labor markets, so in the case of China, it would seem that with such a large population, its industrial base can continue to expand for some time to come. However, in this situation—rapid urbanization and change from an agrarian economy to a capital economy—the key will not be available and affordable labor; rather it will be the more basic problem of available and affordable energy resources. It may even come down to a question of whether energy is available at all, at any cost. As long as the world continues to depend on fossil fuels *and* Asian economies keep up their current rate of expansion, these fuel sources are expected to run out within 25 years or so.

If and when energy resources simply stopped, the immediate effect would be a virtual halt in China's industry. Not only would expansion cease; current levels would have to cease as well. This potential problem would have an immediate effect on the labor pool. Such an outcome would create massive unemployment and an immediate halt to increased prosperity among the working population. In a very real sense, if the economic problems came to pass, they would also be political problems in the complex Chinese culture.

This problem is not limited to energy resources in the form of electrical power. That is a direct and immediate problem of its own. But a closely related problem is China's other resource requirements. For example, estimates are that China's imports of steel are going to grow by 20 million tons per year in the foreseeable future. So investors are not restricted to looking for investments in China. Where are those steel imports coming from? The activity currently is centered in Australia, meaning a smart China play in the future could include investing in steel-producing *Australian* corporations supplying the massive expansion of the Chinese economy.

Raw materials, like energy, are often viewed in terms of how China operates as an export nation. In the United States, where a large segment of consumption of China's manufactured goods is centered, the assumption is that China's production depends on the U.S. consumer. This is only partly true. A healthy portion of China's growth (and related energy demands and needs for raw material imports) is being generated domestically. As China continues to grow and its middle class expands year after year, a growing portion of demand is being generated from the Chinese population itself. Yes, China is expanding as a dominant world exporter, but it is also rapidly growing in terms of its own consumer spending, on domestically produced goods as well as on imports.

The complexities and potential problems in Chinese economic trends present both problems and opportunities for investors. The trend in growth is not limited to manufacture for export but also includes manufacture for domestic consumption. Therefore, predictions concerning expansion (along with energy and resource demands) have several permutations. Growth in domestic consumption depends on healthy industrial expansion, which in turn can continue only as long as the lights can stay on. And of course, if factories cannot continue to produce, that would end consumer spending. It is all related. Given the need for new and expanded energy resources, the new energy technology is a promising sector for future investing. Nuclear energy, hydroelectric power, hydrogen fuels, and liquefaction of coal are examples of promising new businesses. Development of affordable, clean, safe energy sources would undoubtedly represent sound investment opportunities. However, the simple demand for energy does not translate into sure-thing investment profits, for several reasons:

1. *Existing companies may not make the transition.* Consider the case of Big Oil, those companies currently dominating the energy market. Will companies like Exxon be dominant players in the future energy market? They might make the transition and become major players in new energy markets. Chinese equivalents may also be players. However, it is also possible that tomorrow's energy profits are going to be generated elsewhere, so relying on today's oil giants is not a sure thing at all. It is an unknown.

2. *Technology itself may not translate into bottom-line profits.* We have seen it time and again—corporations developing new technology and at the same time not profiting from it in the short term. Investment in research and internal infrastructure may delay bottom-line profits, often for years to come.

3. *Outside forces may impede market value of stock even when profits are earned.* Some companies have dazzling market success but do not reward their stockholders. This results from

outside competitive forces or even from poor management. In some respects, managing the known current status quo is easier and more certain than managing new, rapidly changing market success. The market, that elusive force at work in all of this, is both fickle and unpredictable.

4. *Future change will affect investment value and is impossible to predict.* Any assumptions about potential investment profits have to be based on what you know today. But the future is a different place and, as you know from past experience, the assumptions for all investment decisions will be different as well.

THE FINANCIAL ANGLE—FOREIGN INVESTMENT AND THE FINANCIAL SYSTEM

The banking and currency markets in China, made complex because of SOE problems as well as trends in foreign investment, further complicate the long-term view of China's economic health, and they will also be determinants of how well current growth curves will be sustained.

It is clear that foreign investors are on board with the belief that China is the new investment market. By the year 2002, foreign direct investment (FDI) surpassed $50 billion, a growth rate of over 20 percent per year.[8] This foreign investment is the primary driving force behind China's rapid economic growth. Part of the growth in FDI is subtle, with current investment going more to knowledge-based industry and, more and more, away from labor-intensive manufacturing. This trend is seen on many levels, making the point that while China continues to dominate export markets with its cheap labor and manufacturing-base expansion, it is also competing strongly in other areas, such as IT. In 1997, a mere 13 percent of foreign firms committed advance systems and R&D to their

Chinese operations. By 2001, only four years later, 41 percent were spending R&D dollars in China. Big companies like Motorola, GE, JVC, Ericsson, Panasonic, and Mitsubishi are among these firms. Motorola employed 650 research employees and has $200 million invested in its Chinese research facility.[9] Microsoft is another; it has invested $130 million in its global research center in Shanghai.[10]

This trend demonstrates that, in spite of an oft-held view that China is a center only for cheap labor and manufacturing of denim jeans, tennis shoes, and housecoats, the country is moving forward on many levels. China has already begun to compete with United States and European economics in electronics and technology. Industrial growth in Shenzhen and Shanghai, where IT manufacturing is centered, is occurring at an impressive rate. Shenzhen reported a 25 percent growth rate in nine months of 2002.[11] China's overall exports remain focused on consumer products, but this is changing. In 2002, high-tech products were 20 percent of total Chinese exports, and this area is outpacing most other manufacturing sectors, growing at more than 40 percent per year.[12]

With such growth on many fronts—even in professional services and consulting firms—can the growth rates be sustained? This is the question every investor asks, whether thinking of placing capital in China or elsewhere. The stability of China's currency is central to this question, because the health of the domestic economy depends on continuing interest and investment from the outside.

The SOE problem—remaining a major factor left over from the old system and the topic of gradual transition—does hold down the overall economic growth in China. Although the problem is being reduced over time, it is a slow process. It's not just the state's need to provide monetary support to laid-off SOE workers. To a more serious extent, the SOE and its nonperforming loan (NPL) problems affect the health of the four state-owned banks, which are the core of China's banking system, in many ways an equivalent to the U.S. Federal Reserve System.[13]

Bolstering the big-four banks, China recapitalized this system in 1998 when it issued RMB270 billion in bonds. The following year, additional specialized agencies called asset management companies (AMCs)—specifically, Haurong, Great Wall, Cindra, and Orient Asset Management—were formed by the government along the model of the U.S. Resolution Trust Corporation of the 1980s (which had been established to deal with savings and loan defaults). These AMCs took over RMB1.3 trillion of big-four bank NPLs and began the long and painful process of collections, debt-equity swaps, restructuring, and liquidation—the typical steps required to properly manage defaulted and delinquent loans.

Perhaps the most significant banking reform undertaken shortly after was a significant reorganization of China's central bank and primary banking regulator, the People's Bank of China. Moving away from previous state control and influence over the banking industry, new publicly funded and so-called policy banks were formed. These were the China Development Bank, Agricultural Development Bank, and China Export-Import Bank. Financial historians will recognize a parallel between U.S. banking and Chinese trends, and not in name only. By separating the management of free-market banking (including commercial lending as a core business) from government involvement is an important step. Even so, it is difficult to compare China's financial sector to the U.S. sector. Questionable and even disparate regional accounting procedures and practices bring into question many of the valuation standards employed within Chinese institutions. On a broader level than the analysis of China's financial sector, investors need to be very concerned with identifying the specific accounting standards employed in corporate valuations. This problem is examined in detail in Chapter 5. The point here is that, until a single and consistent accounting standard is developed, comparisons between Chinese corporate standards and the standards in other countries are difficult. In fact, comparisons of institutions within different regions of China may be downright inaccurate.

In the SOE sector, for example, it is impossible to definitively state the level of NPLs with any certainty. The level has been estimated at various times and on different accounting assumptions to reside between 24 and 50 percent of assets.[14] Growth in a corporate sense (not to mention overall economic growth) is significantly inhibited by these chronically high nonperforming rates. If we view these NPLs as a pseudogovernment debt, given the relationship between the banks and the government, they take on a far different face. Rather than thinking of these as comparable to bank bad debts, they may look more like government deficit spending. The hybrid nature of China's economy makes any such comparisons difficult even when, for the sake of comparison, the analogy is accurate.

In the United States, NPLs are a drain on cash flow, but financial institutions often offset such problems by issuing long-term bonds or even additional shares of stock. In China, up until 2002, the idea of selling SOE shares to overseas investors was strictly prohibited—another point supporting the view of NPLs as being more like government deficits than bank defaults. However, this changed, and a financial revolution of sorts has been under way ever since. This involves a redistribution of the estimated $240 billion in SOE share value not available for consolidation, merger, and foreign investment, a massive shift and part of China's long-term transition of the entire SOE structure itself.[15]

CHAPTER 4

EMERGING INVESTMENT THEMES: GLOBAL SUPPLY AND DEMAND

IN ANY attempt to understand how investing in China may work, an outsider has to struggle with the complexities of the Chinese economy and culture. However, it is a mistake to assume that there is only one China. The implications of this are staggering for investors, especially those accustomed to singular markets and investing rules. In practice, China is hardly a monolithic bloc of 1.3 billion consumers, as one Hong Kong–based financial journalist explains:

> It is really a collection of markets in different stages of economic development and with different levels of household affluence. The biggest provinces are virtual countries in their own right. With 74.4 million residents, relatively prosperous Jiangsu, which borders Shanghai, is more than twice as populous as Canada. Guangdong province near Hong Kong is home to another 86.4 million Chinese. The city of Shanghai

(population: 16.7 million) has nearly four times the inhabitants of Singapore. Beijing, the capital, has 13.8 million people, three times the population of New Zealand. Despite efforts by the central government to exert more control, each of the 23 provinces, seven autonomous regions and four municipalities have their own way of doing business.[1]

Any investor who approaches a sector or attempts to time investment decisions in markets outside of China tends to think of the markets as a singular force. Thus, today's bull or bear market would apply universally, even though specific sectors may act or react differently; a specific stock's beta may determine the timing of buy and sell decisions, and the study of marketwide trends may be used to guide investors in managing their portfolios.

Now we come to China, a different matter altogether. Investors need to either view China as a *series* of investment opportunities, often dissimilar or inconsistent with one another, or view sectors (industry-wise and geographically) as entirely separate markets. This is a different view of investing than most investors are accustomed to, but it is a mistake to think of China as a single market, controlled by a single market force or subject to the same rules.

In Chapter 5, the specifics of markets are explored in more detail, including the different stock markets, accounting rules, and other considerations every China investor needs to bear in mind. For now, our concern is focused more on the themes that define the major Chinese investment opportunities in a global sense and that describe China's overall place within the new and emerging world markets. We need to be aware that monetary policies within China and elsewhere are part of a global effect. So valuation of the U.S. dollar, the euro, and other currencies has everything to do with the health of the Chinese currency. The relative investment in debt of other countries is a major factor in China's central banking policy, so investors cannot view this market as entirely separate.

MONETARY POLICY AS A GLOBAL ECONOMIC FACTOR

In the past, investors within a specific market (i.e., the U.S. stock market) proceeded with a sense of isolation. They bought and sold shares of U.S. companies serving predominantly U.S. markets. Any overseas subsidiaries were icing on the profit cake, so to speak, and the focus was on domestic sales and profits. This was the case for decades. In the 1980s and 1990s, a theme began to emerge—global investing or specific investments in overseas markets. This was manifested in specialized international or continent-specific mutual funds, for example, in recognition of the complexities of direct investment outside the United States.

Today, virtually any investor in any country can buy and sell shares around the world through domestic markets. The investment world has expanded sharply to encompass all nations and continents, and, in a sense, to create a single world market in many respects. Ironically, though, although investors may accept this global fact of life when it comes to investing, an equally significant global change is largely ignored: currency policy and exchange.

Is there, in effect, a single world currency today? Officially there is not. Economists compare the U.S. dollar to the euro as a measurement of fiscal health between nations. Until July 2005, China's currency was tied to the U.S. dollar, thus forcing other Asian currencies to do the same. Moves continue to unify currencies among industrialized nations toward single standards—not always quickly or successfully, but the movement is under way nonetheless.

Some historical perspective is worthwhile. Back in 1944, anticipating the importance of postwar reconstruction and economic aid, 44 nations met in the New Hampshire resort of Bretton Woods to design and implement postwar monetary policy on an unprecedented worldwide basis. What has become known as the Bretton Woods Agreement was a revolutionary and farsighted effort at creating an orderly system for the entire world. It was revolutionary because, in the context of the times—with World War II not yet over and before the Cold War had begun—the countries participating in this meeting envisioned a world of international cooperation, trade, and mutual assistance.

Bretton Woods was designed to regulate currency exchange among nations, in order to avoid the chaos and economic disorder that results from depressions, monetary deflation, and the use of fiat money systems. Each participating nation agreed to maintain its currency exchange at a fixed value plus or minus 1 percent, tied to the value of gold, which was a so-called pegged rate. The agreements also established the International Monetary Fund (IMF), which, among other functions, had the role of financing temporary payment imbalances.

Under the agreement, the World Bank was also created to administer, along with the IMF, a series of loans and aid grants to nations to rebuild after the war. The IMF was further to act as the body to monitor and regulate the entire global Bretton Woods Agreement.

The pegged rate of currency designed under Bretton Woods depended on stability in a worldwide reserve currency. In effect, this made the U.S. dollar a sort of worldwide currency because the United States at that time held the majority of world reserves. As a result, the other nations in the Bretton Woods Agreement effectively agreed to peg their currencies to the U.S. dollar, although this was not explicitly stated. Some attendees wanted to create a world reserve currency, notably British economist John Maynard Keynes, but his plan was not adopted. Instead, the U.S. plan, championed by the U.S. delegate Harry Dexter White, won final approval. It enabled the United States to act as the world's major creditor nation and, in the popular view of the time, would ensure U.S. domination of international economic policy for the indefinite future.

To that end, the United States went beyond Bretton Woods, enacting a new law in 1946 called the European Recovery Program and better known as the Marshall Plan. Rather than depending on loan approvals through the IMF, the United States embarked on a series of grants to European nations to help in the rebuilding effort in the belief that such foreign aid would strengthen the cause of world capitalism. Secretary of State George Marshall justified the new law by stating that the situation in Europe required U.S. aid, and that the devastation of World War II was so severe that the new law was urgent:

> The breakdown of the business structure of Europe during the war was complete. . . . Europe's requirements . . . are so much greater than her present ability to pay that she must have substantial help or face economic, social and political deterioration of a very grave character.[2]

The combination of Bretton Woods and U.S. direct aid was supposed to rebuild Europe while ensuring ever-stronger free markets and political stability. The gold standard was the centerpiece of the proposed international monetary stability envisioned under Bretton Woods. Gold had historically been used to back currencies and to settle international debts. As long as all participating nations agreed to live within their means and limit their spending to their gold reserves, the international system might have worked. However, no specific system was built into the agreement for the creation of uniform reserves. It was widely assumed that new gold production would be adequate to finance expansion and new spending.

This plan began unraveling in 1958 when the United States began experiencing a decade-long balance of payments crisis. By 1971, the United States had a reserve deficit of $56 billion and fears emerged that demands for conversion would create a true crisis. In August 1971, President Nixon enacted a number of import surcharges and wage and and price controls, and—most significantly—took the U.S. dollar off the gold standard. By taking this step without consulting the IMF, the State Department, or world allies, the change from the gold standard to a new fiat monetary system doomed Bretton Woods. Numerous other causes added to the demise of the Bretton Woods Agreement and the creation of today's multination fiat monetary system. Most of the world is today off the gold standard and likely to remain there indefinitely.

The dream of an international currency, however, did not really die with the demise of Bretton Woods. In many respects, the industrial nations of the world are, indeed, acting with a de facto world currency today. If you consider China and the United States as the major economic powers today—regardless of where the trends may go in the future—it becomes evident that there is a single, dominant currency in effect. It is more accurate, though, to recognize that by pegging (and now aligning) its currency to the U.S. dollar, China has created an almost universal monetary exchange. The rest of Asia is virtually forced to follow China's example, so that the market consisting of the United States and all of Asia is operating on a single monetary system.

INTERNATIONAL CURRENCY— U.S. AND CHINA AS CURRENCY PARTNERS

A review of Chinese monetary policy requires analysis on two levels: internally and internationally. The People's Bank of China (PBOC), the central banking regulator, has enacted a series of controls and reforms since 1998 in an attempt to ensure stability. Acting much like the U.S. Federal Reserve, the PBOC regulates the economy and monetary policy. It lowered the RMB interest rate nine times between 1998 and 2003 and enabled double-digit growth of China's broad money (equivalent of the U.S. M2) every year from 1998 to 2001, ranging between 14 and 15.4 percent increase. (M2 is the total money supply, consisting of all currency in circulation, amounts in checking and demand deposit account balances in money market accounts, and certificates of deposit under $100,000.) The PBOC has been successful in regulating loans by

financial institutions as well, and has contained deflation while ensuring steady economic growth.

The internal effort at monetary policy has been a great success
in recent years in China. During this time, however, it is also important to consider the economic impact of phasing out the SOEs
and factor in the impact of nonperforming loans as part of the
long-term transition. The PBOC, in fact, has taken steps to eliminate the nonperforming loans over time, issuing RMB270 billion
in government bonds to recapitalize the entire commercial banking
system. At the same time, Chinese economic policy has liberalized
loans to privately owned enterprises where most new employment
is generated, notably in high-tech sectors. Many of these loans are
secured via equity in so-called stock-pledged loans.

The numbers are not small. In the three years from 1998 to
2001, infrastructure and technology loans were greater than RMB1
trillion, consumer loans were RMB699 million, and loans to private enterprise were RMB4.8 trillion, nearly half of all commercial
loans in 2000.[3]

On the nondomestic side, China has derived benefits from pegging (and now aligning) its currency to the U.S. dollar—although
there are risks as well. Having the Chinese currency pegged to the
U.S. dollar allowed China to work in a currency partnership with
the United States, and to enjoy its historical economic strength and
influence. Although it is an oversimplification to merely make that
statement without further discussion, it remains at the center of the
policy decision by China to align its currency closely to the U.S.
dollar, even though it was officially unpegged in 2005.

To ensure that the U.S. currency remains strong, China has
taken steps. It recognizes that the United States is a major consumer
of China's manufactured goods, so it is in China's interest to keep
the U.S. dollar strong and do anything it can to ensure that U.S.
consumers continue buying its wares. As a result, China has become
the largest single holder of U.S. Treasury securities. (Again, this has
to be qualified. By considering China a single economy, we ignore

the multilayered economy of China. The investment in U.S. debt may reside primarily in China's central banking system, but part of the debt includes private enterprise, SOEs, and hybrids of the two.)

However, the extent of Chinese holdings in U.S. dollars and in U.S. debt continues to support the U.S. twin deficits. The budget deficit requires investors to continue buying trillions of dollars' worth of U.S. Treasury securities, and the trade deficit requires continuation of the debt-based consumer buying on the part of the American public.

By the end of 2004, China was holding $120 billion in U.S. Treasury bonds. This number is, not coincidentally, very close to the annual trade deficit between the United States and China, approximating the value of goods the United States purchases from China and in excess of goods the United States exports to China. So the Chinese investment in U.S. debt is directly related to its desire to maintain strong demand for its own ever-growing manufacturing base.

Investors may think of U.S. consumerism as working for Chinese expansion, financing the incredible growth in transportation, urban development, and manufacturing in China since 1970. However, it is not a matter of U.S. interests lending money to China, the textbook version of how one entity invests in another. This transaction is more complex. The United States buys manufactured goods from China, funded increasingly by mortgage and credit card debt (the mortgage and credit bubble), while the U.S. Federal Reserve identifies ongoing consumerism as productivity even though it involves little or no infrastructure investment within the United States. So as the U.S. consumer continues to finance manufacturing growth in China, the Chinese central banking system (primarily, with other China-based interests) finances the ever-growing U.S. budget deficit and trade deficit. These twin deficits are largely responsible for China's growth, representing the market for its goods more than anywhere else. As long as this partnership

continues, the rest of Asia goes along monetarily, and the other major player—the euro—struggles to keep its piece of the pie.

Contrary signs are evolving and may affect both China and U.S.
currency values in the near future. The dollar has been falling
against the euro for the past few years and many have pointed to this
trend as proof that the U.S. economy is about to explode, the dollar
to lose all its value, and the bubbles to begin bursting everywhere.
However, Europe is having problems of its own. The failure of the
proposed European Union (EU) Constitution to gain approval in
France in 2005 (indeed, it was defeated in a landslide condemnation
of the proposal) signals potential weakness in the entire European
system, both monetarily and culturally. This could signal a weakening of the euro in the future, which would shift the advantage back
to the de facto international currency of the U.S. dollar and the
Chinese alignment to the U.S. dollar (as well as the rest of Asia's currencies). Time will tell. For investors, these issues and questions
make it essential to be aware of currency exchange ramifications in
any and all investments. Capital invested in China may be affected
by exchange rates between the major economic centers of the world;
therefore, as a risk factor, currency evaluation is essential.

UNBRIDLED OPTIMISM—
HISTORICAL WARNING SIGNS

The complexities of the intertwined monetary system between
North America and Asia certainly will define the pace and extent of
growth on both continents. No trend continues at the same pace
forever. There can be no doubt that China's economic growth—as
has been the case elsewhere—will have many starts and stops, mo-
mentary setbacks, and inhibiting factors along the way.

From the investment point of view, it is sensible to be on guard
against unbridled optimism. Throughout economic history, such

optimism has led to many speculative bubbles and to the loss of fortunes. Some well-known examples follow.

Tulipmania

Throughout history, monetary, commodities, and stock markets have experienced odd exaggerations. Even in ancient China, over-printing of the first paper money (flying money) eventually caused inflation. More recently, one of the strangest examples of reaction and overreaction originated in sixteenth-century Holland. Tulips were considered to be treasures of beauty and so a commodities market arose. By midcentury, the wealthy classes began investing, preferably in the rarest of bulbs. This went on for decades until, in 1634, ownership of tulip bulbs became a rage. Some prices rose to as much as 5,000 florins for a *Semper Augustus*, one of the more desirable varieties (the same amount of cash could purchase a carriage, a set of horses, and a complete harness set). In one case, a wealthy citizen of Amsterdam offered a 12-acre estate in exchange for a single tulip! In 1636, bulbs began trading on the Amsterdam Stock Exchange as well as the exchanges of other cities. Many people became rich through tulip speculation, but within a short time the entire market collapsed. There was no one left to buy, and the entire system imploded. Difficult to understand in hindsight, such illogical speculative trends are not restricted to the case of tulip bulbs; they occur time and again and will do so again in the future.[4]

Cotton Is King

In nineteenth-century America the economy was largely defined by cotton. Before the discovery of gold in California, cotton dictated matters as the most important commodity. Pre-Civil War Southern prosperity was a direct outcome of cotton harvesting. In 1800, the United States had been producing virtually no cotton at all. By

1860 the South was supplying five-sixths of cotton throughout the entire world—over two billion pounds per year. The cotton industry "was then about as important as the oil industry in the Middle East today."[5] The Civil War years caused a spike in cotton prices, and during that time speculation ran wild. By 1868 prices had retreated and by 1875 they had returned to prewar levels. At one point, it appeared to speculators that endless fortunes were possible, even unavoidable, in cotton. A few years later, many had lost everything.

The Panic of 1907

Two separate crises caused the infamous panic early in the twentieth century. In March, stock market prices crashed, with the Dow railroad index falling from 112.53 down to 99.71 over two days. In October, a money and banking crisis followed, causing yet more stock price panic. As often occurs, the panic fed itself and became exaggerated, then ended as suddenly as it had begun. Numerous domestic and international events have been studied as contributing causes, but essentially the panic could not be clearly blamed on any one event. The fall in railroad and industrial stock prices was puzzling because no reason could be identified to explain it. By definition, the panic itself was irrational.[6]

The Dot-Com Bubble

Although many interim panics have occurred predictably since 1907—including the well-known 1929 market crash, of course—we skip ahead to a more recent oddity, the dot-com bubble. What was so odd about this short-lived and quirky speculative bubble is that the run-up in so many stock prices was based on absolutely no fundamentals. One well-known example, the online bookseller Amazon.com, had never reported a profit during the period that its stock price grew and grew . . . and grew. The president of Amazon,

Jeff Bezos, shrugged off the role of profits in valuation of corporate stock, a conclusion that is amazing on its face. Even Wall Street experts shared this point of view during the dot-com years. The analyst-guru Jack Grubman, who once worked at the big Wall Street firm of Salomon Smith Barney, went on the record saying that the fundamentals—sales, profits, capitalization—had no bearing on valuation, and he derided accounting analysis as irrelevant and a backward-looking method.[7] Thus, the U.S. stockholder created buying demand that ran up shares for dozens of Internet stocks (dot-com stocks), most of which had never reported a profit.

These brief examples of speculative bubbles make the point that history can provide great lessons. It is a mistake to believe that investing in China, or any other market for that matter, is a sure thing, a guaranteed path to riches. There may be fortunes made in the economic changes to come, but just as certainly, fortunes may be lost along the way. That is the cautionary lesson from the past.

MANUFACTURING AS A TIMING SIGNAL

Rather than entering into a fever pitch of speculation and rushing capital into all things Chinese, a more balanced approach makes sense. Investing in China, whether directly or through international managed accounts, mutual funds, or other vehicles, holds great promise for future growth as well as potential risk.

As with all investment decisions, and given the certainty of cyclical starts and stops, investment in China is going to be largely a matter of timing. One of the great indicators concerning timing can be found in manufacturing cycles accompanied by demand for and supply of energy resources (and, notably, future development of new, more efficient energy technology as a door opener to accelerated levels of manufacturing).

Another historical example will help to make this point, even though the pace of historical change was far more gradual than in today's rapidly changing economic climate. In 1885, the United States produced one-fifth of all goods consumed in the world, and this share was growing. Over the following century, the United States grew as a leading economic power and dominated world markets, enjoyed a healthy trade surplus, and controlled most of the world's gold reserves. This wealth seemed permanent and unchangeable, at least until the last 25 years of the twentieth century. So many things changed. China emerged as a competitive manufacturing base with lower wages, aggressive marketing, and savvy business spirit. As China began to evolve from its previous centrally controlled socialist system into a market economy, the competitive spirit came to the front, and China began chipping away at U.S. manufacturing dominance. Today, the U.S. is losing ground and China is gaining.

Does this mean capital should pour into Chinese manufacturing stocks? Perhaps, but not exclusively, and not in every case. Remember, China is really a series of disparate economic entities, with many provinces larger in population and GDP than entire countries. This massive market is actually a number of markets, some healthy and competitive and others less so.

Several factors make the comparison of the United States of the past to China today less accurate. Throughout the nineteenth century, immigration to the United States from both Europe and Asia occurred on an accelerated basis. Opportunities were appealing, and there were not enough workers to let the infrastructure go forward as quickly as desired. This labor shortage, complete with attitudes concerning various people, such as the Chinese or the Irish in one decade or the Italians in another, distinguished what type of work (and wage levels) were to be paid to people of specific racial and national origins. During the entire nineteenth century and into the twentieth century, the shortage of labor was a chronic problem. In China, an odd distinction has to be made.

China's two problems relating to labor involve both a huge population of unskilled and untrained workers, as well as a shortage of *skilled* and *trained* workers in high-tech industries. Just as China as the world's leading coal manufacturer finds it economical to import coal, it finds itself importing skilled labor while its own population is undertrained and unemployment numbers remain high.

This odd problem relating to labor and training is transitional, just as the demographic migration is. China is undergoing a massive shift in social and labor issues as it evolves as an industrialized nation. Unlike the historical growth of the United States, which rarely experienced unemployment problems until the twentieth century, China has to contend with unemployment among previous SOE employees, untrained rural migrants, and existing urban workers who cannot find jobs, while needing to train skilled workers and fill higher-paying, high-tech jobs. We have seen how a small change in population affected economic growth in the past. Building the Erie Canal put New York on the map above the previous commercial center of Philadelphia. In hindsight, it seemed like a small change, but it was significant. As China's modern population migrates not in the thousands but in the millions, the demographic change will also affect the economies of specific provinces and cities within China. This is a reality that most outsiders need to remember and to study when thinking about investing in a particular industry and about where that industry is located within the country.

Three major factors are going to affect how well China makes its complex and multifaceted transition (economic, cultural, and political). The first, the population trend, is reflected in the dual employment problem: unemployment plus unfilled job demand, as well as the ongoing migration from rural to urban areas. The second is financing: No growth continues indefinitely without the capital to back that growth. The third is energy resources, which are finite and inadequate for the continued rate of growth in China. Together, the realities of population, financing, and energy will define the rate of China's growth in the future. None of these will stop or reverse the trend, but all may serve as inhibiting factors.

CHINESE INFRASTRUCTURE AND UTILITY STOCKS— LESSONS FROM THE 1990s

To consider how and when investors may take steps to move capital into Chinese stocks (and before considering the most appropriate vehicle for that) it makes sense to look at the most recent past and to see how investments in China have performed recently.

Many economists have noted that today there are few, if any, long-term investment themes. However, this is not only a current phenomenon; it has always been the case. Anyone who wants to find a true long-term investment—a place to leave money for 10, 20, or 30 years—is going to have great difficulty finding a permanent sector that will dominate growth consistently. A more troubling feature to any investment program is the inability to anticipate emerging opportunities. It is not the lack of long-term investment opportunities but rather the difficulty in seeing what is around the next corner that truly frustrates investors, analysts, and money managers.

In fact, the overall tendency is for the market at large to become attracted to a particular theme, sector, or market long after the maximum opportunities have passed. This is a recurring investment theme. The advice to buy low and sell high may sound sarcastic or even condescending, until you realize that most people do the opposite. The tendency is to buy into markets at their peak (the greed factor) and to then sell in the valley (the panic factor). It is fairly easy to advise others to buy low and sell high, but in practice it is much harder to practice the philosophy. A contrarian point of view is likely to create profits, but it is a difficult theory to practice, requiring nerves of steel and the ability to resist both greed and panic.

If you look solely to research about the past to make future decisions, you cannot make sound judgments about a continually changing present and an unknown future. It has been said that:

> The trouble with research is that it tells you what people were thinking about yesterday, not tomorrow. It's like driving a car using a rear-view mirror.[8]

In the 1980s and 1990s a lot of talk about a new economy centered on Asia. The prevailing opinion was that all indicators pointed up, and there was to be no stopping the emergence of China, Japan, India, and other nations as the new economic world powers.

Investing in China utility and infrastructure stocks in the 1990s appeared to make sense at the time. However, just as Americans who bought railroad, canal, banking, and real estate stocks in the midnineteenth century lost money, those buying certain Chinese stocks in the 1990s also lost. The demand for infrastructure stocks is obvious when the need is great; but that does not mean the trend will last. These projects demand great amounts of capital investment but as development occurs, rates tend to fall. Just as the U.S. railroad industry was largely financed by overseas banking speculation, Chinese infrastructure projects in the 1990s were financed by a similar level of foreign investment. Let us not overlook the facts, however: The English banks that financed railroads and canals lost in a big way more often than not.

Cyclical changes since 1990, not only in China but elsewhere in Asia, have affected the viability of infrastructure, notably in remote provincial sections of the country. A healthy return on investment is never assured with infrastructure projects, because so many outside factors beyond investment and potential return are at play. These factors include inflation, foreign versus domestic investment, gross domestic product (GDP) and other economic trends, and ever-emerging demand. In China, a true energy crisis exists and demand continues to outpace supply. In this situation, the limited energy resources may define the success or failure of infrastructure development and, as a consequence, of investment in such projects.

Logically, investment in energy development, production, and innovation makes far more sense because so much—in some respects, everything—depends on the continued availability of energy resources. An unimaginative viewpoint of this problem would be limited to Middle East oil and other sources of oil and gas. A farsighted view recognizes that emerging technologies and alternative energy sources will define future market growth. China may be heading toward domination of manufacturing industries in the future, but to continue that trend, it will also need to find new energy sources. Related problems—cost, environmental impact, transportation, and international competition, for example—will be solved only by one change, and that is the discovery and development of cheaper, cleaner energy resources.

CHINA AND THE WORLD TRADE ORGANIZATION

The first tendency in the market at large is to discover opportunities only when they have already passed. A second tendency is to think of a sector or a country as a self-contained, isolated investment opportunity. Market isolation was a reality in the past. At the beginning of the twentieth century, there was no widespread automobile and truck usage, and air flight did not exist. So the majority of people rarely traveled more than 20 miles from their birthplace. Comprehending a self-contained and isolated market in those conditions makes sense. Today, though, no country can operate on its own without working through an international economic system.

This need for a global perspective was apparent to Chinese leaders for many years. After 15 years of negotiations, China joined the World Trade Organization (WTO) in 2001. Numerous revolutionary changes have occurred as a result of China's joining the WTO, including opening China's previously closely held banking system to foreign competition. This open market change is scheduled for full implementation by 2007.

WTO membership is a major avenue to attract foreign investment. While China has been undergoing its own internal transition—attempting to phase out the SOE system, notably within its banking structure—it has also been taking steps to encourage a broad spectrum of foreign investment. The changes were requirements for WTO membership, as well as part of the long-term economic transition itself. The changes include requirements for openness to foreign competition and joint ventures; transparency in management and reporting; efficiency in a free market environment; and integrity in reporting, accounting, employee relations, overseas competition, and many other venues. All these changes are occurring, some more gradually than others. These changes are not merely involved with market compliance and rule making; they are part of a more complex geopolitical shift and internal cultural change within China. Again, remembering that China consists of many different sections, economic levels, and methods of working with foreign investors (as well as its own central government), this transition is far from simple.

The significance of China becoming a member of the WTO should be understood in the context of the organization's charter, rules, and influence throughout the world. Increasingly, any country that desires participation in the global economy needs to adhere to the WTO standards and to become a complying member.

Before being called the World Trade Organization (WTO), the member states and related series of trade-related rules, treaties, and agreements were called the General Agreement on Tariffs and Trade (GATT). The name was changed on January 1, 1995. By the end of 2004, the WTO had 148 member nations. Additionally, several nonmember nations have observers at the WTO, many of whom have sought membership. As might be expected, political motivations often cross lines with economic interests, so some nations' applications for membership have been prevented. For example, the United States has blocked Iran's application for membership in the past with the argument that Iran supports terrorism. However, that objection in 2005 became a bargaining chip in attempts to convince Iran to abandon its nuclear enrichment program. In many respects, the WTO theme of trade issues does not take place in isolation from political matters.

The best-known general agreement is that all WTO members are required to grant to other members most favored nation status, which includes provisions such as trade concessions. However, it is far more complex. The WTO provides members with two primary roles. First, it serves as a forum to negotiate trade rules; second, it is an arbitrator for trade-related disputes. This is not without controversy, though. Critics of globalization and specifically of WTO influence believe that wealthy nations and influential corporations exert greater influence than smaller nations or nonmembers, arguing that open market globalization is anything but fair or open. The criticism is not without merit. Nonmember nations are virtually under embargo from world trade in general, and the uniformity of trading rules discourages experimentation. The primary targets of these criticisms are the Big Three of the WTO, the United States, Japan, and the EU. Although this bloc may exert influence over other members, the situation is likely to change as China emerges as a fourth powerful trading partner.

Within the WTO (as well as on its own) China's transition to a major world trading partner is going to be influenced by economic, political, and even military considerations. Reform, undertaken as part of the development of a free market, is a major segment of this, and membership in the WTO accelerates that process. However, several other matters also dominate the agenda, such as the status of Taiwan, relations with the United States (political, military, and economic), and the role China plays with its immediate neighbors.

To a large extent, the emergence of a Chinese market economy is likely to exert great influence on other considerations. Although some nations, notably North Korea, have undertaken aggressive military programs such as nuclear enrichment as a means for gaining advantages in economic terms, China is undergoing an opposite transition. Its transition to a free market economy is likely to reduce the need for (or importance of) a strong military presence in the southern Asian area and will further enhance its global political power and influence. Like any growing nation, China has come to realize that power and influence are more easily gained and kept through strong economic forces than through protective (and expensive) military buildup.

It may seem logical for China to treat its domestic problems as a separate issue from that of global trade. However, membership in the WTO is more than just a necessity in today's global market. In fact, it is likely that WTO membership will directly improve the income disparities between urban and rural Chinese populations. To explain:

> The rural/urban income gap issue may seem a purely domestic one. But WTO will also have an impact on farm incomes that will be both positive and negative. Although some farm prices in China are slightly above international levels, that is largely because production and export subsidies by advanced countries distort international prices and thus, indirectly, contribute to China's low rural income problem. . . . Overall, however, land productivity in China is high, though labor productivity on farms is low as many are under-employed or needed only seasonally. The farm situation also points up what for years to come will continue to be China's biggest single international comparative advantage: the low cost of its industrious, even if largely unskilled, workforce.[9]

This interesting situation—prices affected by subsidies and tariffs—demonstrates how WTO may improve the standard of living among China's poorest sector. However, this will be possible only if China's central government continues to maintain its careful economic balance between subsidizing inefficient leftover sectors (SOEs and their nonperforming loans and chronic unemployment, for example) and some remaining antimarket policies that will gradually disappear as the effectiveness of the free market becomes apparent. WTO membership is a positive step in the right direction.

Even as sensible as it seems all around, China's membership was not a quick or easy matter; it took 15 years to negotiate, primarily because of differences between China and the United States. The U.S. government has exerted its power—not only against Iran and other nations, but also about Chinese entry to WTO—in an attempt to affect human rights policies, military buildup, and many other matters not directly related to trade. This has added tension to U.S.-China relations over the past several decades, and has to some extent defined the relationship, even while robust trade and economic cooperation has continued and prospered. The relationship between these two giants is a mix of competitive—sometimes hostile—spirit and at the same time a type of attraction and mutual respect. This odd relationship crosses economic, military, political, and cultural lines. For example, some sections of the Chinese population were largely unsympathetic to the United States following the tragic 9/11 attacks, but remained very much in love with Coca-Cola, Levi's, DVDs, and McDonald's. Segments of the Chinese population look suspiciously to the United States as an imperial power with evil designs, a view that is a holdover from the days of Mao's regime. At the same time, the desire is there for U.S. technology, human rights, democracy, and free trade.

Some American politicians have at times assumed it was both their right and their responsibility to turn China into a Christian nation, to dictate the terms of trade of all commodities, and treat China as a subservient supplier of cheap goods and labor. Idealistically, the

United States has always believed at the same time that free trade would lead to a free and open market, greater access to democratic law and institutions, and a safer world. So, like China, the United States has held dual attitudes toward the other nation.

It may have been the transition of Hong Kong, as one of the world's great capitalist success stories, when it reverted to People's Republic of China (PRC) control, that had much to do with eliminating mutual distrust and misunderstanding. Some feared that the free market success of Hong Kong would cease once it became part of the larger Chinese nation. Instead, China has expanded free trade zones such as the special zone initiated in Shenzhen. Ironically, the opening up of China economically—including membership in the WTO—is easing tension between the PRC and Taiwan. Some Taiwanese companies have subcontracted assembly operations to PRC-based firms, shifted manufacturing operations there as well, and explored further avenues of trade. It may evolve that profitable trade relations between the mainland and Taiwan may eventually lead to an economic merger, which would prove more significant than actual unification politically.

CHAPTER 5

STOCK MARKETS: DOMESTIC AND INTERNATIONAL

IN THE United States at the beginning of the twenty-first century, it is fair to say that a market and regulatory crisis defined the investment community. A number of high-profile corporate scandals and frauds cost investors and corporations billions of dollars, ended the careers of thousands of employees in dozens of corporations, shattered the reputation and the existence of one of the most prestigious accounting firms, and led to new, sweeping reform, financing of regulatory enforcement personnel on a federal level, and more.

These reforms certainly have redefined investing in the United States. The Sarbanes-Oxley Act (SOX) has affected how corporations interact with auditing firms, how CEOs and CFOs certify statements, who may sit on corporate boards, how executive compensation is determined and by whom, and how accounting firms are allowed to operate.

All of these matters are complex and sweeping, but in the United States one theme remains unchanged: The investment markets, accounting standards, and *rules* for listed companies are identical everywhere. The U.S. market operates numerous stock exchanges and has hundreds of auditing firms for thousands of listed companies, *but the rules are the same for everyone.* This is not the case in China, where standards on many levels vary from one place to another. This is true for stock exchanges, accounting rules, and corporate governance.

A NEW WORLD VIEW:
INCONSISTENT MARKET REALITIES

Investors who are accustomed to operating with a single set of assumptions need to rethink their view if they want to invest in China. Even a flawed system provides a degree of comfort as long as the same rules apply to everyone and are in effect everywhere. So when you face the inconsistency in investment markets that is characteristic in China, it complicates all investment decisions exponentially.

Just as the United States has suffered through a series of crises relating to corporate fraud, so has China. A well-publicized case involved Guangxia Industry Company in the city of Shenzhen. In spite of certification by its auditing firm, the company admitted that it had been inflating profits as much as 400 percent in years prior to 2001. Several other companies admitted to similar problems, including the second-largest financial institution, the Bank of China. Like the United States, the Chinese government has taken steps to reform these problems. The China Securities Regulatory Commission (CSRC) has taken steps to clean up the discovered irregularities and to uncover any others that may continue elsewhere. For example, the regulator has delisted corporations that have not reported profits for three consecutive years, has stepped up its financial examinations, and has made it easier for stockholders to file criminal complaints against management found to have practiced fraud.

Regulatory standards in Hong Kong are higher than elsewhere in China, however. In comparison, the exchanges and corporate standards in Shanghai and Shenzhen may require years of reform to match acceptable standards. A cloud over reform efforts is the state ownership of shares that continues in many cases. State-owned shares are not tradable on the bourses, and the government continued to own shares in many previous SOEs even after they went public. Government holdings are too large to simply sell in the open market without creating a price panic, even though the government may often want to dispose of its holdings. In some corporations, government share ownership represents a major portion of capitalization.

To Western investors, who may view government involvement in the markets as an odd concept—akin to the separation of church and state—the hybrid nature of Chinese markets is difficult to understand. In the United States, institutional investors control the lion's share of the stock market. Thus, pension plans, insurance companies, and mutual funds are the major stockholders in the large-cap markets. However, the government does not invest money in publicly listed companies and, in fact, to do so would be viewed as a conflict of interest. How would Congress vote on matters affecting a corporation in which the government held a controlling interest? How would government intervention in the free market be viewed by the already suspicious public? Given today's mistrust of corporate management and the accounting industry, if the government were involved in equity positions of stocks, it would cause a widespread loss of faith in the markets.

China's markets—like the entire culture and government—are in the middle of a complex long-term transition. This period affects many aspects of life and economics in China, and when it comes to listed companies, government involvement is one of many problems.

Among the problems investors face is the determination of where and how corporate reporting is regulated. In the United States, the Securities and Exchange Commission (SEC) enforces a single set of rules for all listed companies, and state securities agencies have their own rules but operate under SEC-type rules and regulations. In China, a variety of different regulatory standards are enforced. Experienced investors prefer the Hong Kong regulatory environment, which is far different than the same set of rules in other Chinese cities and provinces. In Hong Kong, standards of transparency are more favorable for stockholders than in Shanghai and Shenzhen, where regulation is not as strict. As any investor would also expect, where the regulatory standards are lower, more fraud and corruption will also be found.

Complicating this even further, some companies listed in the Hong Kong market are pure in the sense that they operate there exclusively. Other companies have offices and operations both in Hong Kong and elsewhere within China. As a result, companies with multilocation operations many not be consistently regulated. There have been examples of failed enterprises and branches as a consequence. The problems often are cultural and, as a word of caution, it is a mistake for foreign investors to think of *all* Chinese as sharing the same culture. For example, Hong Kong's culture remains primarily that of a former British colony, whereas mainland China has a series of its own cultural distinctions. One expert provides a warning and an example:

> Hong Kong is not China, as fast-food chain Café de Coral discovered in the 1990s. It had to close unprofitable restaurants in Shanghai, Dongguan and Guangzhou after misreading customers' food tastes and habits. Despite Hong Kong's return to Chinese sovereignty in 1997, the mainland continues to classify the city's enterprises as foreign entities ... this means Hong Kong firms are treated on the mainland on the same terms as U.S. and European companies—as business rivals of domestic players. ... Hong Kong's business people do not really enjoy special advantages in China.[1]

This situation is changing in subtle ways over time, but such change exacerbates the complexity for overseas investors. The situation—regulatory, cultural, and political—is in a state of flux and is continually evolving. It is impossible to define China *today* in terms of how it operated a year ago. Furthermore, Hong Kong is a different China than Shanghai and, in fact, all of the other provinces, zones, and regions. There is no single China nor any single set of rules in force. Investors, therefore, need to define the operational assumptions before determining whether valuation of a listed company's stock is realistic—and whether two or more corporations are valued on the same premise.

The question of accounting standards also comes into play. Levels of regulatory oversight vary from one area to another, and a significant part of that is the question of which accounting rules have been used in setting value. Investors need to ask this question before simply assuming that a series of corporations is all subject to the same rules.

In the United States, it is generally believed that one system—Generally Accepted Accounting Principles (GAAP)—is used for all audited, publicly listed companies. Even with all of its profound flaws, GAAP applies to everyone equally. In China, at least three separate accounting standards may be used in various situations. First, and most conservative, are International Accounting Standards (IAS), which are used as the basis for the very similar Hong Kong Accounting Standards. Some companies listed in Hong Kong are valued based on U.S. GAAP rules, which are far stricter than China's own internal accounting rules.

Are these differences mere nuances? No. The different accounting standards make a considerable difference. Some corporations, in an effort to improve transparency, present three versions of its audited financial statements. Even if the actual earnings are relatively small under these different standards, the fact that three separate standards may even apply is cause for concern. If investors are simply handed three different audited financial statements, how can they conclude that they are actually comparable? Even using GAAP alone, questions have to be asked concerning accounting assumptions; one company may have exceptionally high core earnings adjustments,[2] while another may be more accurate. When this reality is multiplied by the multiple use of different accounting standards, comparisons are made more complex. Any investor making decisions on comparative bases faces a daunting task in Chinese stocks.

CHINESE STOCK MARKETS—CLASSES OF STOCK

Investors approaching the various China markets—using the plural form is accurate because of their complexity—requires studious attention. You contend with varying accounting standards, levels of regulatory oversight, valuation methods, and partial or complete state ownership of stock. Additionally, you will need to carefully study the many variations of ownership form.

Most U.S. investors are aware of the interaction between preferred stock (with its nonvoting features) in various class levels and voting common stock. As complex as the structure of American equity may be, in China it is far more complex. This reflects, once again, the many inconsistent faces of China, even the many versions of the country defined geographically, politically, and, in the case of the markets, by type of share ownership.

There are many different levels of stock involved in various China-based exchanges. Even investors making purchases through managed accounts overseas should be aware of what management is buying in their accounts. First is the A Share, denominated in renminbi value and available only to Chinese citizens and foreign investors through the QFII channel. These shares are listed and traded in the exchanges of Shanghai and Shenzhen.

In comparison, B Shares are denominated in either U.S. dollars (those listed on the Shanghai exchange) or Hong Kong dollars (for stocks listed on the Shenzhen bourse). Chinese citizens with foreign currency accounts, including residents of Hong Kong and

Macau (who are considered foreigners in terms of investment markets) are also allowed to trade B Shares. In addition, certain mainland China shares are traded on the Hong Kong Stock Exchange. These are known as H Shares and are available to all investors; they are denominated in Hong Kong dollars. All shares—A, B, and H—are the same class of shares, just traded on different exchanges.

A limited number of shares are also traded in Singapore (one source refers to these as S Shares). The N Share is ownership of a China-based company that trades on the New York Stock Exchange or NASDAQ, most frequently in the form of American depositary receipts (ADRs). In Hong Kong, traders also trade P Shares, stock in private-sector-owned corporations located in mainland China. However, it is important to note that the nature of share structure and share ownership is changing fairly quickly in China. The capital market regulator, the China Securities Regulatory Commission, has introduced a number of reforms in recent years and plans to further reform the system moving forward. These reforms relate not only to share structure but also to limits on foreign investment.

At present, however, it is necessary to describe entire classes of stock based on ownership, location, type of company, and where they are traded. First are the red chips, corporations incorporated in Hong Kong that operate as units or subsidiaries of mainland Chinese firms owned, in one form or another, by the government (central, provincial, or ministerial). The red chip corporations operating outside mainland China gradually purchase the assets of the state-owned parent companies in exchange for China Depository Shares. Serious concerns about corporate governance, regulatory oversight, and the accuracy of valuation of mainland corporations—even those privately owned—have led many investors to prefer buying shares only in those corporations that trade outside mainline China. However, given the complexities of exchange between parent and subsidiary, or between SOE and private ownership, there is not always a clear dividing line. Steps under way to simplify classes of stock include current reforms aimed at merging A Shares and B Shares into a single class.

Cesar Bacani, in his book *The China Investor* (John Wiley & Sons [Asia], 2003), coined the term *purple chips* to describe H share stocks that trade as red shares in Hong Kong and that have the potential to become what in the United States would be called blue chip companies. Bacani has suggested that the combination of red chips and H shares may become standard in the future, and he classes this group of companies as purple chip stocks. The distinction of this group is a fast pace of current growth: consistent profitability and earnings growth, cash dividends, professional management (even those state-owned purple chips may be professionally managed), audit by reputable auditing firms, and accountability to a strong regulatory oversight system (such as those in Hong Kong and the United States). Bacani also observes that under his definition the stocks should be tracked by major brokerage houses, thus making them visible as potential candidates for institutional investors in the United States and elsewhere.

In short, purple chips will contain the same fundamental positive attributes as similar companies in the United States that pass essential fundamental tests. The further qualification that such companies should also be audited properly and subject to regulatory oversight may surprise many Westerners, where such requirements are automatically assumed. However, a distinction between a U.S.-style blue chip and a China-style purple chip has to include assurances that valuation is reasonably accurate. Given recent corporate problems in the United States, it is clear that this issue should not be taken for granted, even though it has been in the past. China is not alone in having to deal with fraudulent management, corruption, and exaggerated earnings. However, the purple chip stocks, by definition, would be the Chinese equivalent of a U.S. value investment, defined by tests of fundamental and capital strength (and augmented by qualification about how valuation was arrived at in terms of audit and regulatory environment).

Bacani does not stop at the distinction of purple chips. He also explains what a green chip stock is and what this means.

They are in many ways the equivalent of what U.S. investors would call a start-up company, a penny stock, or an initial public offering (IPO). These three terms have some definitive crossover meanings, but they are not mutually exclusive. In China, green chips are the stocks of relatively young ventures. Bacani qualifies them by pointing out that these companies may be undercapitalized and thus could have problems attracting debt capitalization within China. Management may be inexperienced in the importance of corporate governance. In spite of the capitalization and regulatory disadvantages, this range of potential investments, much like U.S. upstart corporations, tends to excel in comparison with larger SOEs. In China's emerging and restructuring economy, green chips may outperform the average company. It is an environment perfectly suited to entrepreneurs and innovators of many kinds. Brokerage houses and institutional investors are not likely to pay much attention to green chips due to their unproven value, inexperienced management, capitalization limits, and other fundamental problems. However, it is equally likely that as time passes, some brokerage firms will develop indexes to track groups of emerging, privately owned stocks, and exchange-traded funds (ETFs)—mutual funds traded on public exchanges and involving a pre-identified basket of stocks—may focus on green chip type stocks in China as growth continues.[3] However, the overall mutual fund business in China's various markets remains in its early phases, unlike the high popularity funds enjoy elsewhere. This situation is changing rapidly, however.

EMERGENCE OF CHINA'S STOCK MARKET

As we have seen, the majority of available shares in China (A Shares) can be traded only by Chinese residents, so the market is not yet fully open to foreign investors. This is likely to change over time, probably more rapidly than most observers believe.

To put the situation in perspective, we may learn a lot from observing stock market history. In the United States, the stock market has not always been open to the general public; in fact, the whole concept of owning stock is a relatively new one. Trading in stocks can be traced back to 1725. In those days, New York's population was about 35,000 and only professional dealers were able to trade stock among themselves. There was no market for public investment. After the Revolutionary War, trading in securities became available to individual speculators (as well as bankers, politicians, and anyone else) in the form of government bonds. The first U.S. Secretary of the Treasury, Alexander Hamilton, came up with the idea of selling "War Bonds" to pay off the large war debt accumulated by the newly formed nation. Shortly after, the First Bank of the United States was formed, and it sold stock to financiers, brokers, and public officials. Again, few unconnected citizens took part in the speculation.

The organization of early stock exchanges set down rules for brokers and dealers to trade among themselves. While they often managed funds for banks and institutions, their activities were usually for their own accounts. In fact, the first known agreement, drawn up in 1792 (for the organization that eventually became the New York Stock Exchange), was formed specifically to spell out how brokers would deal with one another and to eliminate the auction process, and also to set a commission that would be charged to companies for transacting their stock.

The following 100 years were characterized by widespread speculation in canal and railroad stocks, as well as overseas banking interests and commodity price movements, notably in cotton. Other than a few individual speculators, the focus on trading remained exclusively among brokers, financed by institutions and financiers. The general public had no part in the business of the stock exchanges, at least not directly. Anyone with the money to buy and sell stocks had to depend on brokers to do their trading for them. It was only in the post–Civil War era that individuals first gained direct access, usually through speculative schemes and often driven by exceptional events like the discovery of gold in California, the fall in share values of railroad stocks, and changes in cotton prices due to farm implement inventions. From 1860 to 1900, much manipulation occurred in stocks, and speculation was more common than long-term investment. Railroads dominated; in fact, as one market historian described the situation, railroads were spreading "like measles at a girls' boarding school."[4] Railroads were primarily responsible for the expansion of the exchange system, and the invention of the stock ticker in 1867 finally opened up exchanges to ordinary citizens.

The stock ticker was a revolutionary invention. It enabled individuals to trade in stocks for the first time. They did not need to visit the stock exchange directly (and, in fact, they could not get in to trade, since brokers held a monopoly on all direct trading). The ticker opened up the exchanges and the entire securities market. The ticker had as much impact in the United States from 1867 onward as the telephone would have a decade later and—more importantly—as the personal computer and Internet are having on the markets today. The big difference is that while the stock ticker opened up U.S. markets, the Internet is opening up global markets.

The stock ticker, invented by Edward A. Calahan of AT&T, not only opened up the markets to individuals who wanted to trade securities, it also presented new opportunities to speculators and con artists. In 1869, for example, infamous manipulator Jay Gould used stock ticker technology in an attempt to corner the gold market. So just as the Internet today has opened up global trading to virtually anyone with a home computer, the stock ticker improved market access in its day, while also making it easier for some people to more efficiently control the market. Calahan's invention was later improved upon by Thomas Edison. This led to the development of the Universal Stock Ticker. At the same time, Edison was also working on a transmittal device called a Private Line Printer. As a form of dedicated communication working through telegraph technology, this device could be considered a nineteenth-century forerunner of today's Internet.

The point here is that the nineteenth-century developments such as the stock ticker and the telephone made the markets accessible to *everyone* for the first time. The brokers' dominance of trading for their own accounts up until that time kept average people out of the markets. The lack of efficient or instant communication prior to these advances would have made individual trading cumbersome and untimely in addition, so there were practical constraints. However, once the technology became available, people became interested in trading directly. Brokers began working for individual accounts in their trading activity. Even so, it was not until the 1990s—more than a century later—that it became possible for individuals to place trades directly from their home computers using online trading services.

In modern-day China, you see remnants of an outdated brokerage system. Only a few years ago, trades had to be done in person and were limited to relatively few floor brokers. Even with the advent of automation, resistance to change delayed full automation for several years, and it was not until recently—after the start of the new millennium, in fact—that fully automated trading was allowed on China's exchanges.

ALTERNATIVES FOR INVESTING OVERSEAS

With the current state of China's stock market in perspective, in Part II you will find ideas and suggestions concerning the specifics of moving capital into China-based investments. The following section is a broad overview of the many ways that you can invest in China and of the resources available to you.

Brokerage Firms

The trading system in Hong Kong is fully automated but by U.S. standards it remains quite slow. The modern exchange has been fully operational since 1994, when an outdated system was replaced. Under the old system, brokers had to manually match trades in person or by telephone, and then the final trades were input to a computer system, where buy and sell orders were matched. By today's standards, this procedure was the dark ages of trading procedures, but, even so, Hong Kong–based brokers resisted the change, fearing it would diminish the value of their trading seats. When off-floor trading was finalized by the end of 1996, off-floor activity had already accounted for more than half of all trades executed.

Other changes have occurred to modernize Hong Kong's trading procedures. As recently as 1994, maximum orders of 100 board lots were enforced, and they were only increased to 200 early that year. The current AMS/3 system enables brokers to connect directly to the floor for the first time, and there is no longer a requirement for a floor broker to manually approve and enter electronic orders. Today, on-floor trading accounts for only about 3 percent of all turnover, and trades in which both buyer and seller are on the floor physically are down to under 1 percent.[5]

Although this pace of change may seem slow, it is important to recall that the system in the United States is not that far ahead. In the mid-1980s, for example, order placement was done in person or by telephone through physical brokerage offices, which, in turn, had to make separate contact to specialists and floor brokers at exchanges. Chronic problems, such as unavailability of brokers, the inability during heavy trading to get through on the telephone, and mix-ups in order execution, were commonplace until the late 1980s. Hong Kong's system may seem ancient by U.S. exchange and trading standards, but the system in use today is only a few years behind the U.S. system and very likely to catch up within a few years, at the most. The day is coming when international exchanges will all operate with the same level of efficiency, especially when employing online trading capabilities.

As of 2003, according to author Bacani, his office computer in Hong Kong has been connected directly to his online broker, just as would be the case in the United States. He explains that his broker's

> site interfaces directly with the Hong Kong Stock Exchange's AMS/3 trading system, so my orders get into the queue fairly quickly. (The Hong Kong bourse allows only one transaction per second for every seat held by an Internet brokerage, compared with hundreds of transactions per second per gateway in the U.S.) My broadband connection ensures that my computer also communicates at a fast clip with my broker's website.[6]

Although the U.S. system is more efficient today due to higher volume of transactions allowed, it is clear that Hong Kong's system is not far behind. In fact, there is no technological impediment to bringing the system up to match U.S. standards. The only actual issue preventing this today appears to be a lingering hold on the part of old-style brokers, who are not yet willing to relinquish their physical exchange control and influence to automation.

Investors working through international brokerage affiliates (for example, with offices in New York or London) have a far easier time working through online brokerage firms tied to the Hong Kong Stock Exchange than investors in other countries. For example, investors in India, Malaysia, Japan, Indonesia, the Philippines, and Thailand (as well as most European and Latin American bases) can trade only in *local* stocks through their exchanges and brokerage houses.

A variety of direct online Internet brokerage outlets are available for investing in China. These include the following:

HONG KONG:

> Boom.com—http://home.boom.com.hk
>
> HSBC Broking Service—www.broking.hsbc.com.hk
>
> SHK Online—www.shkonline.com
>
> DBS Vickers Securities—www.dbsvickers.com
>
> KGI Asia—www.kgieworld.com

SINGAPORE:

> Phillips' Online Electronic Mart System (POEMS)—www.poems.com.sg
>
> Lim & Tan—www.eq.com.sg

U.S. BROKERAGE FIRMS OFFERING INTERNATIONAL TRADING SERVICES:

> Charles Schwab & Co.—www.schwab.com and www.schwab-europe.com
>
> Harris Direct—www.harrisdirect.com
>
> e-trade—https://uk.etrade.com

PART II

METHODS AND STRATEGIES IN THE NEW MARKET

CHAPTER 6

AN INVESTOR'S ROAD MAP INTO CHINA

A NY INVESTOR embarking on a new program—whether product specific or country specific—is invariably going to face numerous problems. Cultural, political, and monetary barriers arise inevitably, not to mention unfamiliar accounting, trading, and valuation rules.

As demonstrated in Part I of this book, investing in China is a daunting task. With the numerous separate trading platforms and rules in different cities, investors outside of China need to realize that there is not a single China; each stock exchange, province, and overall region is subject to its own set of rules and variations. This chapter provides a resource for you in your quest for valid and updated information, investment advice, and a worldwide expertise that is going to be difficult to find elsewhere.

In the recent past, China has had to deal with six primary inhibiting factors in expanding its markets. As you research this market, it is useful to track reform progress in six areas:

1. Poor corporate governance and performance.

2. Inconsistent policies.

3. Conflict among government agencies.

4. Nonfloating shares (the degree to which is critical in assessing valuation).

5. Restrictions on foreign investment (check share type and changing trends).

6. Market manipulation.

Even though China and its stock exchanges are making rapid progress in all of these six areas, they may continue to serve as inhibiting factors to some degree in the near future. Another issue important in judging China's economy and market is the supply and demand of market capital. This requires a study of institutional investors, both within China and internationally, corporate balance sheets and valuation, and the status of nonperforming loans among previous SOEs (and where those bad debts or late-performing loans have been moved). Another comparison relating to capital where China looks healthier, economically speaking, than the United States is the private savings levels. It is ironic that old stereotypical views of China and its demographics persist in countries like the United States. The Chinese worker is viewed as an uneducated rural person willing to work in a sweatshop for pennies per day—a view that is far from the modern-day reality of the fast-growing Chinese middle class. Savings rates comparisons between China and other industrialized nations make the point that China is rapidly becoming a *fully* industrialized nation. While poverty does persist in many rural areas and problems continue in terms of training, unemployment, and previous SOE employee transitions, change is taking place very quickly—and this has positive ramifications for investors.

GROUND RULES FOR INVESTORS

A few guidelines for anyone embarking on a new investment venture:

1. *Work with experienced and knowledgeable advisers.* The first basic requirement for success is that you identify the right

people for the job. For example, you would not hire a real estate attorney to handle a patent question or a divorce, nor should you retain an investment advisory firm with no experience (or research capabilities) in China. Although this may seem basic and obvious, many investors depend on their existing stockbroker, financial adviser, or financial planner for all of their needs, even when that person or firm may not be qualified to offer sound advice. Loyalty is an admirable trait, but it can be expensive.

2. *Consolidate your research and advisory services if appropriate and when possible.* The difficult matter for investors approaching the China market is the complexity and multi-layered research required. This refers not only to picking a good investment, which is the premise on which most people start. In the case of China, you have to also consider the attributes of each stock market within the country, accounting standards, economic considerations for particular sectors, design and ownership of each class of stock, and the array of cultural, political, and philosophical complexities involved when investing in China. For all of this assistance, you need to use an advisory and research service that can offer you all that you need from a single source. Otherwise, any investment program will be chaotic and may result in information gaps, conflicting advice, or time delays in the important decision-making process.

3. *Match your requirements to what providers offer.* No two investors have identical requirements, risk tolerance levels, or investing goals. Thus, you should seek advice from an individual or firm that is a good match for you. A diversified company offering a range of services relating to investment research, fundamental and technical analysis, and updated news and information is invaluable. Matching what is offered to exactly what you need is the key.

Collectively, these guidelines may seem unrealistic. Why? In some countries, investors have become accustomed to one-size-fits-all advisory services. Sadly, the U.S. market is a typical example. In recent years, the newspapers have been full of disturbing headlines about abuses by publicly listed companies and their management, by accounting firms, and by investment brokerages houses as well. Not only do many of these corporations apply formula marketing strategies, expecting investors to pick from what they offer instead of tailoring programs to individual needs, but they also have done a poor job of protecting their clients' interests.

Many investors in the United States have become cynical, because recent disclosures have shown that, time and again, the traditional establishment of brokerage firms has betrayed the public trust. Consider the stream of news in 2002 reported in the *Wall Street Journal* to understand why investors have become dubious about the advice they receive from brokerage firms:

May 23—Investor complaints against brokerage firms rose in one decade from slightly more than 4,000 in 1991 up to about 6,500 by mid-2002. Problems include theft of clients' funds, shoddy handling of accounts, pushing underperforming stocks, and other activities that clearly were not part of providing service to investors.[1]

June 5—One of the largest Wall Street firms, Salomon Smith Barney, acted as lead underwriter for Adelphia, but the SEC investigated the brokerage firm for possible conflicts of interest and considered whether it had violated securities laws.[2]

July 17—The major Wall Street firms and their stock ratings were compared, with the conclusion that the ratings system was a waste of investors' time. Recommendations to buy were common, but recommendations to sell were rare, a study found. Six brokerage houses were studied. Although Morgan Stanley's percentage of sell ratings was 20.9 percent, the remaining brokerages were suspiciously low. Merrill Lynch's sell ratings were only 5.8 percent of total recommendations; Prudential's, 3.5 percent; Goldman Sachs's, 1.0 percent; Lehman Brothers', 1.0 percent; J. P. Morgan Chase's, 0.9 percent; and Credit Suisse First Boston's, 0.4 percent.[3]

October 31—Ongoing conflict of interest among big firms offering both underwriting and advisory services was highlighted with mention that recommendations to buy continued to dominate analysts' positions. Even though attempted reforms were in place, the conclusion was that "Moves to split analysts from bankers won't end conflicts, but investors will likely pay higher fees."[4]

It should be shocking that so many problems plagued the big Wall Street firms in 2002. It is even more disturbing that the problems appear to continue today, even after multimillion-dollar fines were imposed on these brokerage firms. But is this the status quo for investors in the United States, where people use the services of numerous companies, and numerous branches within companies, and transparency is in many ways inadequate? In fact, an October 2002 survey—conducted while the widespread scandals and brokerage audits were under way—revealed that 63 percent of Americans expressed a belief that American financial institutions were not able to protect them against losses and fraud. Another 31 percent also said they had completely given up all hope for the U.S. system. In the survey, trust in stockbrokers was lower than trust in insurance salespeople, truly an indictment of the entire profession.[5]

GUIDELINES FOR INTERNATIONAL INVESTORS

In approaching the complexities of investing in China, virtually every investor outside of that country will need assistance. Investments will have to be made domestically (in the United States, for example) through mutual funds and other managed accounts operating under the U.S. regulatory umbrella, or with the assistance and advice of an experienced investment research service. This is the topic of Chapter 10 of this book. For now, the following six guidelines are offered for anyone interested in working with a service for investment in China.

1. Is your advisory firm knowledgeable and experienced about investment selection in China?

In selecting a domestic advisory service, the first step is to ensure that the company selected knows the Chinese investment landscape and is able to match the appropriate investment program with your risk tolerance level. A one-product-fits-all strategy will not work, because Chinese investing involves (1) disparate stock exchange and regulatory standards, (2) various accounting and auditing standards, (3) a number of different classes and types of stock, and (4) sectors that operate not only in the normal industry-specific sense, but also in vastly different regions of China.

2. Does your advisory firm have China-specific experience and knowledge?

An advisory service should be aware of how different industries operate, of course. But in the case of China, it is also important to know how industries are affected by their locations. Are factories and offices found in largely rural areas, in Shanghai, or in Hong Kong? How does this affect the valuation of a company's stock? How reliable are audited statements? Is any portion of the stock owned by the state or by local governments, and, if so, how much do they hold? What are the growth prospects for a company based on these factors?

3. How sensitive are specific sectors or companies to outside factors?

Some industries are sensitive to changes in interest rates and other economic forces. In the case of China, what happens to a company if the U.S. dollar's exchange value falls, or if the U.S. economy suffers a new recession? How will the company be affected by changes in the commodities market and in specific commodity prices?

4. What is the plan for diversification of your portfolio?

It never makes sense to invest everything in a single stock; it is also unwise to put all of your portfolio in the stocks of a single country. The amount to allocate in China depends on your and your advisory firm's perspectives about risks of particular stocks or sectors, the allocation balance in your overall portfolio, and considerations about how much, if any amount, you allocate to stocks of other overseas corporations. This decision also depends on the vehicle you select—direct stock ownership in domestically listed corporations (i.e., on a U.S.-based exchange) or through traditional mutual funds or an exchange-traded fund (ETF)—and on the type of investment (stocks, commodities, precious metals fund, or index, for example). In other words, any percentage identification would be arbitrary, since every investor has to consult with his or her advisory firm to make that decision.

5. Have you defined your objectives and, if possible, diversified between value and growth issues?

The growth trend in China has been spectacular and is likely to continue on some level and for some time to come. But as with all growth trends, you cannot know exactly where or for how long, so a two-part strategy makes sense. It is prudent to identify value stocks based on the traditional fundamental tests (of course, after qualifying that the audited accounting standards in the stocks you review are consistent and based on either U.S. GAAP or international and/or Hong Kong conventions). These tests should include a consistent history of cash dividend payments, low to moderate price-earnings (P/E) ratio, and healthy sales and earnings trends. But in making these fundamental analyses, remember that the comparative standards may not be reasonably compared to stocks in your country. For example, U.S. P/E ratios may be considered favored when at or below 20, but in China, higher overall growth expectations may take average P/E ratios higher. This means stocks might be more expensive, but those price levels may be justified by greater growth potential. So the growth and value equation can work together. If you prequalify companies based on fundamental tests and then identify the most promising growth prospects, you will be more likely to pick stocks with the greatest investment potential.

6. Have you compared transparency and regulatory oversight for companies?

It cannot be emphasized enough that selection of stocks in China involves an array of different markets and a variety of standards. Thus, you or your advisory firm should pay careful attention to who manages a corporation, and make sure that a high standard of transparency is at play. For example, corporations that willingly publish their financial results based on all three accounting standards[6] are disclosing more than may be required under regulations; this is a positive sign. Also be aware that not every company in China is subjected to the same high level of regulatory oversight as is applied to Hong Kong–based corporations.

AN INTELLIGENT APPROACH TO THE NEW MARKET

Naturally, all investors will be wary of new markets, especially those outside their home countries, those subject to unfamiliar rules and customers, or those based on entirely different assumptions than they are accustomed to. When investing in China, either directly or indirectly, numerous considerations have to be remembered. The following five sections summarize the discussions of these considerations from previous chapters.

Volatility and Future Uncertainty

All growing markets go through periods of volatility, not only in market price, but also in the fundamentals such as sectors and market leaders, and rule-making or policy-related issues. In the case of China, tremendous changes have occurred over the past decade, just in the details of how markets operate. It is only fairly recently that transacting has become fully automated, moving away from the outdated requirement that a broker physically handle and approve all transactions. The maximum transaction volume is growing steadily. As China's markets move rapidly toward domination of worldwide stock trading, you will see further changes, and with those changes greater volatility will be experienced.

The growth-related volatility may be temporary, an attribute of transition. However, for investors, future uncertainty is a far greater potential problem. Markets do not like uncertainty, and in the case of China there are so many uncertainties—political, cultural, demographic, economic—that it is impossible to know exactly how much growth to expect or how quickly.

Potential for Growth and Inhibiting Factors

Most future-looking experts anticipate incredible and rapid growth in China. They may be right, but you should not forget that many of the same predictions were being made in the 1980s and 1990s regarding Asia-wide growth. Today, those predictions have quietly moved to focus on China as the leading economic force in Asia, and none of the predictions foresaw Japan's troubles. Therefore, it is reasonable to expect growth but, at the same time, many of China's specific problems will act as inhibiting factors. These include unemployment, the need for training, energy shortages, and the ever-present political realities of China in its massive transitional period. Growth will occur, but its pace and success will be limited by the many inhibiting factors that also need to be overcome.

A related potential inhibiting factor is the unreliability of the economic numbers themselves. The complexity of China makes it difficult to define the country economically. In economic terms, China is really a series of quasi-independent provinces, cities, and economic zones, each with its own economic challenges and problems. China's published economic data have been notoriously unreliable. For example, the true national debt for China usually excludes SOE debt, which should be included. GDP numbers may be unreliable as well. Even unemployment cannot be counted realistically, due to the large-scale underemployment problems in China's poorest rural and agricultural regions. These unreliable statistics make it difficult to estimate likely growth patterns on underlying assumptions familiar in the United States or Europe.

China's Multilayered Transitional Culture

Several transitions are under way in China beyond the specific changes under way in stock market rules, corporate transparency in financial reporting, and access to overseas investors. All of these transitions affect current and future investment opportunities and risks.

Demographics

The physical movement of massive numbers of people presents a challenge to the Chinese government. As millions of people move from rural China to industrialized China, all wanting jobs and housing, China faces the problem of what to do with unskilled and untrained workers. The availability of millions of new workers enables China to compete on one level, specifically in manufacturing. Chinese industry is able to produce goods in demand in the United States and elsewhere for a fraction of the labor cost, and this is a significant advantage. But it has a downside as well.

Poverty

Those Chinese living in poverty resent the fact that so many resources go to industrialized and urban areas. The poor are untrained; and there is only slow movement toward filling the training gap. While China grows internally, its millions of families want housing and automobiles and other conveniences. China is becoming an industrialized nation, but it is a mix of rich and poor.

Employment

A four-pronged challenge faces China today and in the future. The most visible of these is unemployment. Millions of untrained rural families have moved to the south and coastal areas in search of jobs and a higher standard of living. But the numbers usually don't count the underemployed in rural areas, where year-round productivity on small farms in particular translates to income levels that do not sustain families. The third serious challenge is the need for training. While China faces a large unemployment and underemployment problem, it also lacks skilled higher-level technical workers, and government and industry have both been slow to fix the problem by instituting serious training programs. Finally, there remains a core of previous SOE workers who remain unemployed. Many of this group resist reeducation because of their age (they tend to be older workers) combined with a mind-set left over from a state-controlled economy. Under the communist system all workers were employed by the state, and today the remaining SOE sector is far behind the productivity curve of the nation as a whole. The laid-off workers previously employed in SOEs were guaranteed lifetime security, so they are having difficulty accepting the limitations of unemployment, the change in the structure of their lives, and the insecurity that goes with those changes.

SOE Transition

Even beyond the SOE-based unemployment problem, the transition from SOE to privately owned companies is slow and painful.

The SOE sector remains large and many companies are hybrids, partially state-owned or state-controlled and partially private. The transition affects the economic numbers as well. The nonperforming loans of SOEs are huge and add to the realistic national debt in China. The low productivity and high unemployment associated with SOEs, and the often long delays in paying workers, demonstrate that many labor problems and economic questions remain. However, China can complete its transition only gradually. The SOE sector is an oddity that has grown from the transition away from state control toward free markets. It is not a simple matter.

Free Markets

The Chinese corporate and business community is embracing the free market and rapidly learning to thrive within it. Even so, this transition is long term, and many people in China (including SOE employees, many older government workers and politicians, and the more conservative communist interests) resist the changes, even though the widespread success of the free markets has improved the standard of living for millions of Chinese families. The point is that any controversy about the logic of moving toward free markets is gradually evaporating but, at the same time, resistance has to be expected.

Energy Shortages and Alternative-Energy Development

One serious impediment to growth remains energy-related problems. Some parts of China face periodic blackouts. During high-consumption periods some factories are required to close and houses can go dark. The demand at this point is simply far greater than the supply. When you consider the energy demands of any industrialized nation and how widespread and all-pervasive those demands are, it becomes quite clear that China's growth will be limited to the extent that it cannot meet its energy demand.

Stock Exchange Rules and Investment Restrictions

For most investors living in the United States and Europe, the rules of stock exchanges are fairly uniform and well understood. However, in China, each exchange has its own rules and these may vary considerably. The situation is even more complex. There are so many classes of stock, each with its own restriction on who may own and trade, that for any foreign investor expert advice is essential. No foreign investor would be wise to simply begin moving funds to China and buying stocks directly.

Accounting Standards and Variance in Valuation Assumptions

A related problem involves the complexities of how companies are valued. In the United States, the well-known GAAP standard is flawed and imperfect, but it is applied to all listed companies and used by all auditors. In Europe, a stricter standard is applied, also uniformly. In China, at least three accounting standards are used. It is impossible to compare two or more corporations without also ensuring that the financial statements those companies publish have been prepared on the same basis.

There are promising signs. Chinese regulators are working hard to provide investors with transparent disclosures. Some corporations have begun publishing audited financial statements prepared on all three accounting standards, so that investors can make more informed decisions. This idea would vastly improve matters in the United States, but the accounting industry has yet to address all of its conflict of interest problems.[7] However, there is a new Global Uniform Standard for the reporting of financial statements known as XBRL (eXtensible Business Reporting Language) that companies such as Microsoft and General Electric (GE) have voluntarily adopted. This standard is being actively promoted in China, and it is hoped that this may become a solution to the issue.

CHAPTER 7

DEVELOPING A CHINA STRATEGY

ALTHOUGH YOU need to accept the possibility that things may change rapidly (in China or, for that matter, in any market), it remains an exciting prospect to diversify a portfolio to include equity positions in the rapidly emerging market of China-based stocks. The venue may include mutual funds and exchange-traded funds (ETFs), overseas indexes, or purchase of stocks listed on U.S. exchanges (directly or through American depositary receipts). To invest, however, the critical importance of research—from expert, knowledgeable professionals—cannot be overstated.

To find the best advice as to how to proceed, you need the expertise that comes from an organization providing on-site knowledge about the Chinese market (not to mention the Chinese culture, political environment, and economic conditions). For this level of help in what is essentially an investment new frontier, you cannot look to long-standing domestic companies for help. They are simply not equipped to advise you.

Besides locating expertise with offices within China as well as around the world, you need to be able to identify a range of stocks, mutual funds and ETFs, and other alternatives that will place your capital in the China market. In the following chapters, these questions are addressed specifically.

MUTUAL FUND AND ETF
ATTRIBUTES AND SELECTION

The rather sudden emergence of China as an economic world power has taken many segments of the investment world by surprise. It was only a few years ago that there were no high-rise buildings in China, few automobiles, and virtually no home computers. Today, China is, at least in the industrialized and urban areas, a modern country.

Even so, the complexity and risks remain. It's likely that many individual investors who find the China market interesting will stay away nonetheless. This may occur due to complex differences in accounting standards, regulation, and classes of stock. There is a solution for you if you fit into this group, however. It is possible to buy into the China market through a diversified portfolio—even a small one—by using mutual funds and the even more flexible variation, ETFs.

In fact, mutual funds present solutions for many investors. Those who would prefer to make a play in a specific market, but who want broad exposure, may prefer an index fund (either in the China market or elsewhere). Hedge funds are appropriate for those anticipating changes in price direction marketwide. Balanced funds continue to provide a mix of equity and debt that, in the case of China, opens up many interesting possibilities. Finally, the traditional growth fund is a long-standing favorite among investors and one that is also likely to perform well in the rapidly expanding China investment world.

Why are mutual funds so popular? Less than a century ago, mutual funds didn't even exist; today, mutual fund assets total $6.3 trillion. The size of funds has expanded more than 200 times in the past 23 years. For example, in 1978 total mutual fund assets were $34 billion, less than one-half the size of many of today's bigger mutual funds.[1]

Within China, mutual funds have been rapidly growing since

their introduction in 1998. In only a few years, the industry has grown manyfold, measured by the number of funds and by assets under management.

Recognizing that there may be many venues for anyone to invest in China, it remains a basic necessity that the risk features of all investments be kept in mind. Mutual funds may serve as a method to achieve diversification and asset allocation at the same time, while avoiding the risks associated with buying stocks and bonds directly. In fact, for investors residing outside China, direct purchase of securities on the China stock exchanges is considered by many to be impractical and high-risk. These specialized markets are more logically approached through domestic markets with expertise in foreign investment, conduit products such as mutual funds that are recommended by expert investment research sources, and domestic companies that invest in China and elsewhere outside of the individual's home country.

In addition to the high risks associated with direct investment, international restrictions on capital transfer and holdings of foreign securities are an additional inhibiting factor. Citizens of a specific country are often prevented from moving large sums of money to foreign accounts. This restriction is made even more complex by the potential losses from currency exchange rate differences over time.

For the vast majority of investors managing their own portfolios, some level of mutual fund investing makes sense (even if limited to money market funds so that temporarily idle cash continues to earn interest). This is a means for spreading risk and for ensuring that some portion of the portfolio is protected against the potentially damaging effects of sudden and unexpected price changes. However, in the past most investors have viewed mutual funds in purely domestic terms. Even those intent on allocating funds overseas have used domestic-based mutual funds specializing in foreign investing. This remains an appropriate avenue for investing in China. However, the mutual fund market is also changing as investing becomes international in nature, and as the markets begin to expand physically and via the Internet.

The international expansion of markets is ideally suited to pooled products. Mutual fund investing is becoming more popular than ever today and your choices within this industry are growing exponentially. As the demand for index funds and especially for the relatively new ETF market grows, the variety, size, and investment value within the industry will continue to grow as well. For the China investor, mutual funds in various configurations may be the most practical, affordable, and safest port of entry.

In any market such as China's, it is realistic to expect some volatility in the short term. This is, of course, both an opportunity and a risk. Some stocks, sectors, and industries are going to go through various changes. Long-term potential may be elusive, and you may determine that professional management of funds is necessary in the China market.

Investors living outside of China, who probably are not familiar with how the market works, are going to be better off using professional advice through an experienced investment advisory firm; domestic investment services specializing in the China and Asian markets, including research-based professional services; and finally, mutual fund management. The experience and track record of a fund's management are the starting point for qualifying a mutual fund. After all, you will be paying a fee to management to make wise investment decisions; their experience and history reveal whether they have selected a portfolio wisely.

In all cases of mutual fund investing, the basics are worth keeping in mind for product selection. These basics include the following seven points, some of which we will develop further:

1. History and performance.

2. Size in terms of assets.

3. Management.

4. Costs and fees.

5. Net asset value and trend.

6. Other attributes.

7. Investment objectives.

Costs and Fees

In connection with costs and fees, it is important to become familiar with several terms and concepts:

- The *expense ratio* is a comparison between ongoing expenses (including management fees, administrative expenses, shareholder servicing, and 12b-1 fees), divided by average net assets. Fees vary considerably. One study indicated that funds with assets between $1 billion and $87 billion reported average expenses ratios of 1.07 percent, and smaller funds— those with assets between $100 million and $500 million—reported ratios averaging 13.7 percent.[2]

- Included in the expense ratio are *management fees* or, putting it another way, compensation of the team deciding where to invest money. The amount of fees is disclosed in the portfolio and a comparison is worthwhile.

- Funds are either *load* or *no-load*. The load is the amount of commission taken from invested assets to pay a salesperson. In theory, you pay a load in exchange for an adviser's expertise in picking the best fund but, in fact, the best fund yesterday may not perform as well tomorrow. No-load fund shares are purchased directly from the mutual fund rather than through the broker. With over 10,000 fund choices, some investors consider the sales charge a good investment; for others, the deduction of as much as 8.5 percent of all funds invested is simply too high and not justified. For example, for every $100 invested in an 8.5 percent load fund, only $91.50 actually goes into the investment; the rest goes to the salesperson. Studies between the two groups indicate no long-term advantage of load funds over no-load funds. So investors seeking advice are better off finding a fee-based financial planner and paying a one-time consultation fee, then buying shares directly in a no-load fund. If you are going to invest $3,000, a consultation fee of $200 for a one-hour analysis will be less than the initial load charge, so this is a worthwhile alternative to paying 8.5 percent on *all* the money you place in load mutual funds.

- *Back-end load* or *deferred sales charges* are fees that are invisible when you initiate a program. For example, if a fund charges a deferred fee, all of your initial investment goes into the fund. But you are charged a fee when you sell shares. Some funds will assess this fee only if you sell within a specified period of years.

- The *12b-1 fee* is an oddity. Even some no-load funds assess this hidden load charge. It is named after a provision in the Investment Company Act of 1940 that allows funds to charge a fee for marketing expenses. It was authorized by the SEC in 1990, ostensibly to help investors. The argument is that marketing of a fund helps current investors, and that selling more shares increases the net asset value. In practice, however, there is no specific benefit to current fund shareholders; the 12b-1 is simply a hidden load fee and nothing else. The maximum annual 12b-1 fee is 1 percent of asset value and, as a general rule, most of this money goes to paying brokers.[3] These fees are worth avoiding, so even when limiting a comparison to no-load funds, it is equally important to avoid any mutual fund charging a 12b-1 fee.

Other Attributes

Is a specific mutual fund open-ended or closed-ended? A variation on the closed-end concept is a hybrid being seen more and more. Many open-end fund managers have come to recognize the problems of managing exceptionally large amounts of assets, so they close the fund to new investors. Existing investors are allowed to continue investing more, but no new money will be accepted. This limitation on growth is a positive step for existing fund shareholders.

Another variation on the classification side is the index fund. In the case of the China investor, the large numbers of indexes lend themselves to an array of index fund choices, either via traditional routes or through ETFs. An index fund works like the traditional fund that picks a portfolio of stocks, bonds, or a balance of each. An index fund divides its assets among the constituents of a specific index, duplicating the performance of the broad index itself. In the United States, for an example, a popular index fund involves purchasing all of the S&P 500 stocks. A growing number of index funds specialize in other market indexes and, in the case of China, the base of China stocks and bonds is rapidly growing as well.

Investment Objectives

The final distinction among various funds and other pooled investments is the all-important investment objective. There are several variations, including:

- Growth funds: aggressive, moderate, or conservative.
- Income funds: equity growth funds, bond funds, tax-exempt bond funds, unit investment trusts, balanced funds, option income funds.
- Real estate investment trusts (REITs) are not mutual funds, but a type of pooled investment specializing in the real estate market: equity, mortgage, and hybrid REITs.

- Mortgage pools: The best-known mortgage pools are the Federal National Mortgage Association (FNMA, web address www.fanniemae.com), also known as "Fannie Mae," and the Government National Mortgage Association (GNMA, web address www.ginniemae.gov), or "Ginnie Mae."

- Variable annuity: The variable annuity is a hybrid product including features of mutual funds and life insurance annuity products. The annuity aspect provides tax-deferred income and a death benefit, while the mutual fund aspect gives you diversification, flexibility, and professional management. The variable annuity is popular in structured retirement programs.

- Specialized funds: Mutual funds may also specialize in methods other than the distinctions between growth and income. Traditional mutual funds investing in *international stocks* may further be subdivided by country, region, or sector. Domestically or internationally, *sector funds* isolate their holdings to specific market sectors only. Some funds limit their investments to *small-cap* or *special situations*, even to buying shares only in *socially conscious* companies. An array of more finely tuned specialized funds may also be found. For example, within the sector fund classification, funds may specialize in utility stocks or energy stocks only. A *flexible portfolio fund* is designed to shift among stocks, bonds, and the money market, depending on overall conditions. These may also be called *asset allocation funds*.

Most of the highly specialized funds and other pooled investment programs require little in the way of management because portfolio decisions are defined in advance. So as a fund investor, you may ask the legitimate question, "Why am I paying for management in these circumstances?" The ETF alternative (explained later in this chapter) provides all of the advantages of mutual fund investing for lower costs, and often with more flexibility.

MUTUAL FUND ACCOUNT MANAGEMENT

As an investor in a mutual fund, you need to decide not only what kind of fund to purchase, but also how to manage your account once you decide. For the array of decisions you need to make, using professional help is a logical first step. However, remember, this does not mean you have to pay a load to get good advice. Paying a one-time fee to a fee-based financial professional is a wise method for identifying one or more no-load funds or ETFs that will meet your requirements.

The management decisions you will need to make can be divided into four specific types. Each is discussed in the following sections.

Investment Amount and Frequency

Some fund accounts can be opened for minimal initial investment levels, such as $100. Others may require relatively large initial investments, such as $5,000, required in some specialized funds and mortgage pools. Subsequent investments are also subject to minimum requirements. Many investors want to set up a program involving periodic withholding from their paychecks, with funds deposited each month into mutual funds. Some traditional savings programs were established to invest as little as $25 per month. Today, many funds require higher minimum investment levels, simply due to the administrative cost of managing thousands of small incremental transfers. So in picking a fund, the initial investment minimum and subsequent minimum levels should be one of several criteria for picking an appropriate fund.

Reinvestment of Earnings

You have a choice in mutual funds of taking your earnings in cash payments or reinvesting them in the purchase of additional shares. So capital gains, dividends, and interest can be paid out or left to accumulate at compound return rates. Some people want fixed income, so they select income funds and depend on periodic payments. Others can afford to leave earnings on deposit where they grow at ever-accelerating rates and "interest on interest" (the effect of compounding) grows over time.

Tax Planning

Whether you take income in cash payments or leave it on deposit to purchase additional shares, you are taxed on your earnings each year. You may have current income (dividends and interest) or capital gains (short-term and long-term). Those buying shares in tax-exempt funds will not be taxed; and dividends, if qualified, are taxed at a lower rate than ordinary income. For investors with high taxable income and large mutual fund holdings, the tax treatment of income is an important aspect to fund investing.

Some tax shelter is possible. Buying a variable annuity creates long-term minimum return promises, a death benefit, and tax deferral of earnings; and the diversified mutual fund portfolio is structured within the variable annuity as well. Shelter is also achieved for high-income investors through tax-free bond funds. Although municipal bonds are exempt from income tax, they yield less than market-rate bonds. A study of the net tax income is important to determine which route makes sense based on your individual tax rate.

Diversification within Fund Families or between Funds

Holding shares in a single mutual fund provides one form of diversification. The portfolio itself is spread among many stocks so mutual fund investing is efficient and convenient. However, many investors want to also split their funds between growth and income, or between aggressive and moderate growth objectives within funds. For those requiring some liquidity, some portion of investment capital can be placed in a money market fund, where it can be accessed via a checkbook. So if you select a "family of funds," it is possible to diversify among several different funds. This can also be achieved by buying shares of funds offered by many different companies.

Diversification can be accomplished in many ways; but the complexity of working with many different companies should be considered when determining exactly how to proceed in a program of diversification or asset allocation. In the interest of spreading risks, it is all too easy to set up your portfolio so that its sheer complexity offsets the advantage of spreading the risk.

MUTUAL FUNDS IN THE CHINA MARKET

The complexities of the China market will draw many investors to index investing and to mutual funds (both traditional and ETF types). When you consider the alternative of buying shares of stocks on a one-by-one basis, selecting mutual funds to diversify China holdings offers a number of advantages:

1. *It overcomes the problem of capital transfer.* For most people outside of China, transferring capital directly into overseas markets is complex for several reasons. Among these is the simple restriction or extra regulatory aspects of moving capital away from domestic markets. Such investors also have to be concerned with currency exchange rates, safety of capital, and uncertainties about foreign regulatory oversight.

2. *You may rely on research and management for traditional funds.* The traditional mutual fund has to be assumed to work under

professional management. Picking a fund managed by experienced analysts and experts should do the job of selecting the best stocks for a portfolio, even when those stocks are concentrated in a foreign country. Investors in mutual funds, by definition, pay for the expertise and they expect that their capital will be wisely invested by the fund's management.

3. *You may rely on the diversification of indexed ETF funds.* For the ETF market, there is no need to rely on management's expertise. Rather, you buy an ETF to track a specific index (or sector or geographically distinct group of stocks). So by choosing the ETF with its preselected portfolio, you can efficiently diversify capital into the identified basket of stocks.

4. *Choosing pooled investments based on indexes is the best form of diversification.* As efficient as the ETF format is in terms of diversification, the most efficient way to enter the China market is through an ETF tied to an index such as an FTSE/Xinhua index. The methodology used for such indexes, in which weighting is monitored to ensure fairness, provides investors and associated ETFs with high-quality standards.

5. *You avoid the complexity and market risk of a complex multi-layered Chinese regulatory and auditing system.* For investors outside of China, a number of potential problems arise when considering investing, including (1) inconsistent regulatory levels by city, zone, and province, (2) several dissimilar auditing standards, (3) an array of different types of shares and stock classifications, and (4) potential problems in making comparative analyses on valuation of company stock.

INVESTING VIA EXCHANGE-TRADED FUNDS

Exchange-traded funds are relatively new and may revolutionize the entire mutual fund industry. The popularity of the mutual fund market has been a huge success story; but even with its practical advantages, diversification, and convenience, there are other choices. An ETF is an investment company whose shares are traded on stock exchanges at market prices. The ETFs available in the market at present follow stock indexes; that is, they invest in the stocks in a particular index.

Like other index funds, the portfolio is identified in advance and, in fact, defines the ETF itself. So an ETF designed to track the S&P 500 will always contain shares of all of the S&P 500 stocks. And an ETF identified as one investing only in gold mining stocks will contain investment shares in a short list of companies engaged in gold mining activity. Similarly, an ETF that follows an index of Chinese stocks will invest solely in Chinese companies. No discretionary powers are held by management, so the corresponding management fees are far lower than those in traditional funds.

Beyond open-end, closed-end, and bond funds, newer products have included umbrella fund families, guaranteed funds, money market funds, ETFs, and direct or pooled futures trading. By the end of 2004, the full range of stocks, funds, bonds, options, and futures was available to some degree; the breadth of all of these markets and their availability to individual investors grow more with each passing quarter. Funds are a key component for any investor who wants to be involved in the China market. Only local Chinese residents are allowed to purchase A Shares, and the numbers demonstrate that A Shares are, in fact, the lion's share of the overall China market, a potentially serious restriction for anyone outside of China. For example, by mid-2003, capitalization of China's stock market consisted of just over US$500 million in A Shares, and less than US$200 million for B Shares, H Shares, and red chips combined. Because trading in Chinese A Shares stocks is restricted, most individual investors are excluded from direct ownership of the largest market portion. So for many of these individuals, investing in the broad China market has to be achieved through purchasing shares in index funds, mutual funds, or ETFs.

Why the popularity in this new market? There are many reasons, not the least of which has been the poor record of many traditional managers. By far, managed funds have performed below market averages, so astute investors have lost faith in the concept that in some way a team of experts gains a market edge. In fact, it appears that the exact opposite is true. An ETF is described as holding a basket of stocks identified as having attributes in common. The only changes to that basket would involve a change in the attributes themselves. For example, if a stock falls off of the S&P 500 and is replaced with another, the ETF will sell its shares in the previous company and reinvest in the new one. In fact, the oldest ETF is the S&P 500 Depositary Receipts (SPY) fund. This fund was formed in 1994 and has shown over time that the ETF can be more tax efficient than other types of index funds. Over its first 11 years, SPY averaged capital gains distributions under 0.02 percent, compared with an average of 0.52 percent among the three biggest S&P index funds.[4]

Another ETF advantage is that funds are kept closer to 100 percent invested. Traditional mutual funds are required to maintain cash on hand for redemptions, but ETFs are not. So more of your money is at work and the overall returns will be higher as a result. But perhaps the most intriguing aspect of the ETF is that shares are bought and sold on the stock exchanges just like stocks. Traditional fund shares have to be bought and sold through the fund's management, but ETF investors can buy and sell online with a keystroke and, although a transaction fee will apply, it is far more convenient and efficient.

Expense ratios have shown to be far lower in ETFs than traditional funds, primarily because there is no need for professional analysts and managers. For example, many of the larger ETFs report expense ratio as low as 0.2 percent. Traditional funds generally assess expense ratios between 1.0 percent and 1.5 percent.

For those investing relatively small increments of capital, traditional mutual funds may continue to provide lower commissions and, in the case of no-load funds, no load fees whatsoever (compared to ETF transaction charges). However, for those with a higher volume of investment capital, the ETF is clearly more efficient and cheaper to own. One exceptional feature not available with traditional funds involves option trading. Many ETFs allow investors to buy and sell options on the ETF itself just as you can on individual stocks. This opens up a window of opportunity (and risk) not available to traditional mutual fund investors. Although options are complex, investors familiar with the market may view this feature as one of the most important. Options cannot be traded on all ETFs, just as they are not available on all listed stocks. The ETF market is very young. As at July 2005 there were 171 ETFs in the U.S. market, 46 of which followed global or foreign indexes.[5] However, ETFs are continuing to grow and, for many investors, they offer an avenue into specialized sectors and countries that would otherwise not be available.

Investing in any market—whether in China or elsewhere—demands careful and thorough analysis. Highly specialized alternative investments, including options, futures, and American depositary receipts (ADRs), are not suitable for everyone. The levels of risk in certain strategies, the special trading rules, terminology, and capital requirements all require a higher-than-average level of experience and investment sophistication.

THE OPTIONS MARKET

Options are among the most complex of investment products, and not appropriate for everyone. This does not mean that options are automatically unsuitable for you if you have never traded them in the past, however. Anyone can begin a program of options trading by studying the market and learning how options function within it. There are many strategic uses of options beyond mere speculation. Any brokerage firm (whether online or not) is required to ensure your suitability before allowing you to trade options.

Brokers may be useful sources for information and guidance. But remember, even those who understand the basics may not be familiar with the special rules involved in trading options on China markets. These rules may include timing of trades, methods of execution, the ability to close a position before expiration, and even the very basic level of risk exposure involved in particular strategies. Because Chinese stock exchanges do not all operate under identical trading rules, the complexity is expanded when you try to gauge the market and trading rules within those different exchanges. When you overlay these special concerns onto the complexity of the China market, it becomes clear that options trading is not for everyone.

Some questions should be asked and answered as a starting point:

Can You Trade Options in Chinese Stocks?

Options can be traded in China in a variety of ways—directly on individual stocks or on a variety of indexes and ETFs, both through exchange listings and through brokerages. Because the specific procedures may vary among China exchanges, many investors will find it safer and easier to trade options on China-based indexes and ETFs, and to execute transactions domestically. One important aspect of trading options is timing, and the complexity of international trading makes direct involvement inappropriate in some situations.

What Is the Best Venue for Such Trading?

Options are available on only a few indexes and ETFs. For investors interested in tracking and investing in the broad China market, indexes are the intelligent choice. For those who want to leverage capital at the same time, options are one avenue worth pursuing. This market enables you to limit risk exposure as well as leveraging capital. However, this is appropriate only if you also are willing and able to accept the risks.

Should You Trade Options on Individual Stocks or on Indexes?

Some investors prefer trading options on individual stocks. One problem with trading options on stocks is that there are relatively few available today. The stock-based options market exists in China, but several problems have to be dealt with. First, this is a very new market, so it is limited in scope. Second, the nature of trading options on stocks directly is highly specialized and time sensitive, so investors (especially those interested in speculating with options) cannot efficiently work through third parties, such as brokers or financial advisers. The problem is made more severe by the issues of time zones and international communication. Finally, direct involvement in options trading in China requires virtual on-site involvement. As with most other types of investments, gaining direct access to the China exchanges is a problem and not for most investors. This leads most people, logically, to an alternative: trading options on China-based indexes or restricting stock option activity to the short list of Chinese companies that are listed on U.S. exchanges and that also offer options.

For the more speculative options trader, the China market may not provide the kinds of opportunities sought in this market, at least not yet. The entire options trading capability in China will require a few more years of regulatory development, automated trading systems, and international and perhaps multi-exchange listing facilitation. All index trading is, by definition, broad; thus, you are not likely to gain large profits by trading in the index market. So for options traders who want to pursue individual stock option trading, the question comes down to how and where to make those trades.

AN OVERVIEW OF OPTIONS TRADING

Anyone considering using options as part of a China investment strategy needs, as a first step, to create an overall strategy. This has to consider the international implications of the investment program, the location of the appropriate support staff, research into the specific markets (Hong Kong or other China exchanges), and trading venues you want to explore (direct purchase through China exchanges or domestic exchanges).

Once you have narrowed down the strategic and locational questions of your investment plan, you should then consider whether to use options. This should be based on your level of experience in the options market, risk tolerance, investment goals, and whether you are making your own decisions or working with a professional adviser. The options market is not one in which a novice should depend on an option-savvy stockbroker for advice; it is not as straightforward as buying shares of stock. In fact, if an individual were planning to depend on the expertise of an experienced options broker to make trading decisions, that point of view would normally disqualify the person from trading options. The only sensible method for an individual lacking direct experience to buy and sell options would be through an options mutual fund or an appropriate hedge fund. Some funds are set up specifically to buy stocks and sell covered calls, for example, and this is one example of how an inexperienced investor can become a player in the options market without direct knowledge of the market itself. Otherwise, the best advice for inexperienced investors is to stay away from this market until they have performed more research, have gained approval for some very basic options trades, and have become well versed in the complex options terminology that defines this market.

OPTIONS ON INDEXES AND ETFs

The best-known form of options trading relates to individual stocks. Increasingly, option activity on indexes is becoming the trading method of choice, especially in specialized markets. Because it is possible to write options on indexes and on some exchange-traded funds, this is becoming a method for diversification, without requiring purchase of mutual fund or ETF shares. Investors who either speculate on individual stocks or employ options for insurance, for leverage, or to create current income can employ a variety of advanced strategies.

Options can also be bought or sold on a variety of market indexes. The rules have to be checked in advance to ensure that you know how exercise is accomplished, because some indexes are set up American style whereas others are European or capped. This variation can apply in any market within China or elsewhere, so anyone buying or selling index options should first check the rules of the exchange and for a particular index.

Investors can also trade options on some ETFs, but not on all of them. In the case of the ETF market, investors should determine the availability of options and exercise and expiration rules for each ETF that offers options trading. Because both indexes and ETFs do not experience the same volatility in price movement as is possible on individual stocks, the entire experience of trading options is likely to be different as well. With single stocks, option speculators may purchase calls or puts in the hope that prices will move rapidly and substantially, and they will be right some of the time. However, the highly volatile price movements most desirable for option speculation are not as likely in the case of index and ETF options. Because the indexes are made up of a number of stocks and because ETFs have broad portfolios, volatile price movement is far less likely. Speculation in index and ETF options is subject to a more stable series of trends.

ADR TRADES—ANOTHER ROUTE

American depositary receipts (ADRs) are yet another type of product that foreign investors can employ to make a play in the China mar-

Among the web sites devoted to ADR listings, information, and links for additional information, the following are worth checking:

JPMorgan/Thomson Financial—www.adr.com

Bank of New York—www.adrbny.com

Citibank—wwss.citissb.com/adr/www

International Assets Holding Co.—www.intltrader.com

ket. They are available for more than 60 Chinese companies. ADRs are specialized money market instruments that overcome the complexity of monetary exchange. Companies outside the United States that trade on U.S. markets are denominated in ADRs rather than in the currency of the host country or U.S. dollars. Thus, ADRs serve as an alternate form of currency for international markets. The ADR is a receipt for foreign corporate shares held by U.S. banks. Just as U.S.-based stocks may be held in street name rather than investors taking stock certificates, the ADR is an international version of the same basic concept: They make trading easier by allowing companies and shareholders to trade easily and efficiently on U.S. markets. So for all intents and purposes, ADRs themselves are traded just like U.S.-based stocks. As the value of the U.S. dollar versus foreign currencies changes, the ADRs' value will change as well (because they represent equivalent U.S. dollars). If the U.S. dollar declines against a foreign currency, the value of the ADR would rise, and vice versa. Because the ADR is a money market instrument whose value is not fixed, money market speculators and investors may buy and sell ADRs separately from their denomination for stock trades.

The ADR was first introduced in 1927 to facilitate investment on foreign shares. Today, three levels of ADRs may be issued. These are:

Level one: The basic and simplest form of ADR is used for foreign countries that do not qualify for a listing on a U.S. exchange. These ADRs trade over the counter and meeting SEC requirements for this level of listing is fairly easy.

Level two: These ADRs are either listed on an exchange or quoted on NASDAQ. They also have higher trading visibility than level one ADRs.

Level three: The greatest prestige is held at this trading level. Whereas levels one and two are designed for exchange-based trading, level three is a variation on the public offering. The issuer makes a public offering of foreign-stock ADRs on a U.S. exchange. Because level three ADRs involve raising capital to place investment issues, they also attract money market and stock speculators and investors alike, and they may demonstrate the greatest trading activity on the NYSE and other U.S. exchanges.

The ADR enables individual investors to buy shares *directly* in a foreign company and to trade shares on a U.S. exchange. This alone overcomes the most overwhelming aspect of foreign trading involving direct ownership of shares. The complexities of currency exchange, foreign trading rules, and restrictions on movement of funds between borders keeps many would-be investors out of the market, and ADRs overcome that problem. This is of particular interest to anyone who wants to own shares directly and who is not interested in investing through international mutual funds or ETFs or in using index options.

For the issuing company, the ADR expands the potential investor market outside the host country. It provides a truly international market of potential shareholders and allows companies in countries like China to raise capital for expansion without the limitations of a local economy and capitalization structure.

The ADR, like most products, is not without risk. Some important forms of risk have to be considered for anyone thinking about buying stocks in Chinese companies by using ADR-denominated shares on U.S. exchanges.

The exchange rate risk is perhaps the most serious form of risk beyond the ever-present market risk that all stockholders live with. The ADR value fluctuates with changes in exchange rates, which, in turn, also affects valuation of shares held via ADR denomination. Even though China's currency rose in value only marginally when it unpegged from the U.S. dollar in July 2005 (on the first day of the new policy the yuan rose by just 2 percent), this could change in the future and the yuan could rise substantially. Indeed, many observers believe the yuan is undervalued by anywhere between 10 percent and 15 percent. If or when China's currency value changes significantly relative to the U.S. dollar, share values on U.S. exchanges would be affected as well.

A second form of risk is inflation. Here again, all stockholders are concerned with inflation, and when it comes to international investing, inflation risk is a direct outgrowth of exchange rate risk.

Valuation risk is a special concern when dealing in China stocks. You need to be aware that valuation and accounting standards are inconsistent among markets, so before picking any ADR-denominated stock based in China, you need to determine which accounting standards were used. By making like-kind comparisons, selection of stocks can be done realistically whether you are comparing Chinese companies or comparing China-based to domestic companies. However, without determining the basis for valuation, you have no way to know whether the fundamentals are developed on the same assumptions among different corporations.

Political risk also should be considered for any form of investing in China. This is especially important for ADR-based stocks because, as money market instruments, these will be particularly quick to react to exchange rate adjustments. The fact that speculators in the money market may further influence the value of ADRs adds complexity to the political risk.

STOCKS LISTED DIRECTLY ON U.S. EXCHANGES

Beyond the ADR market, some investors may find it advantageous to own shares directly in Chinese companies that are listed on U.S. exchanges. Some of these duplicate the companies on the ADR list, but many are available in U.S. dollars, just like domestic companies.

As with any selection of stocks, investors should examine the financial statements of the companies in question, determine accounting methods employed to set valuation, and apply fundamental and technical tests in selection of stocks to make informed decisions. To view annual and quarterly reports and filings with the SEC, the companies that list directly on U.S. exchanges can be examined by going to their web sites or by using one of the free annual report sources available online.

CHAPTER 8

AN ANALYSIS OF CHINESE STOCKS AND FUNDS

C HINA'S ECONOMIC growth over the past few years has been nothing short of extraordinary. The country's gross domestic product (GDP) has remained more than double that of the United States, while export and import levels have been rising significantly for some time. While the Chinese bonanza has benefited other countries and economies all around the world, it has not come without concern. The Chinese government has introduced a number of measures over the past year to apply the brakes to the country's economy, and these have had mixed effects on the stock markets. Some Chinese companies and industries have done well; others are now feeling the heat.

So exactly how much is the country's economy growing? Official Chinese figures place the GDP growth in 2004 at 10 percent, and according to the Asian Development Bank (ADB) it was 9.5 percent. Some investment banks, however, have put the real rate at one or even two percentage points higher. In comparison, GDP was 4.4 percent in the United States, according to official U.S. government estimates. Whatever the true figure of China's GDP growth rate, and despite efforts by the government to apply the brakes, the economy is still roaring along. Again in 2005, according to ADB figures, China's GDP was 9.4 percent in the first quarter and 9.5 percent in the second quarter.

With this sort of growth, the government has been under increasing pressure over the past couple of years to place the economy in a position of more sustainable economic growth over the long term and to curb inflation. A large part of the growth has been driven by loans by banks to industry as well as by booming export levels (even though China has been importing huge amounts of commodities to fuel its growth). With this in mind, the government over the past year introduced a number of measures to slow these two economic drivers. The China Banking Regulatory Commission, which supervises the banking and financial industry, increased the capital requirements for loans, raised lending standards, and increased its scrutiny of lending. In July 2005, the government revalued the Chinese currency, which, among other effects, could slow exports.

PERFORMANCE OF KEY INDEXES

Any measure to cool down the economy is destined to have an impact on the stock markets. Some companies, including banks, property companies, and major exporters, have seen their share prices affected by the changes. Others, however, have felt little impact. Accordingly, some of the key indexes trended downward in 2005, while some headed upward (see Table 8.1). The most often quoted Chinese index, the Shanghai Composite Index, an index of A and B Shares of major Chinese companies, fell quite considerably—by 8.33 percent—in 2005. However, in comparison, the most quoted Hong Kong index, the Hang Seng, rose 4.49 percent over the same period. Moreover, the FTSE/Xinhua China 25 Index (FXI25), an index of China's top 25 companies, rose 10.63 percent in 2005, and the rise continued into 2006 (see Figure 8.1).

This impressive rise for the FXI25 is consistent with the index's performance over the prior three years (see Figure 8.2).

TABLE 8.1 PERFORMANCE OF KEY U.S. AND CHINA INDEXES, JANUARY 2005 TO DECEMBER 2005

Key Index	Jan. 3, 2005	Dec. 30, 2005	Rise/Fall	Rise/Fall %
FXI25 (TRI)	9,393.41	10,745.01	1,351.60	14.39%
FX125 (PI)	8,318.99	9,203.65	884.67	10.63%
Hong Kong Hang Seng	14,237.42	14,876.43	639.01	4.49%
S&P 500	1,202.08	1,248.29	46.21	3.84%
NASDAQ Composite	2,152.15	2,205.32	53.17	2.47%
Dow Jones Industrial Average	10,729.43	10,717.50	−11.93	−0.11%
Shanghai Composite Index	1,266.50	1,161.06	−105.44	−8.33%

Prices quoted are closing prices.
Date: February 15, 2006.
Source: Xinhua Finance/Mergent Analysis.

FXI25 PI = Price Index
FXI25 TRI = Total Return Index

FIGURE 8.1 FTSE/XINHUA CHINA 25 INDEX, DECEMBER 2004 TO FEBRUARY 2006

Source: Xinhua Finance.

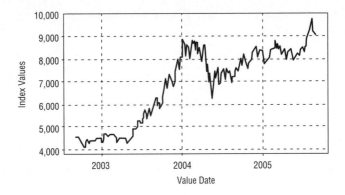

FIGURE 8.2   FTSE/XINHUA CHINA 25 INDEX, AUGUST 2002 TO AUGUST 2005
Source: FTSE.

Some analysts have attributed the falls in some markets to the government's efforts to curb growth as well as the result of increases in oil prices—a development that will hit China the hardest, given it has been one of the fastest-growing consumers of oil and gas over the past year. At the same time, some industries are not likely to be hit hard by the changes the Chinese government has introduced; in fact, some may even benefit. Such variations reinforce the value of closely scrutinizing particular indexes and particular stocks for the best performers.

OPTIONS INDEXES ON CHINA STOCKS

At the time this book was written there were few China-related indexes in the United States on which options could be traded. With more China stocks being traded on U.S. exchanges, this is likely to change in the future. As with investing in any product that holds investments in a number of stocks, it is wise to investigate the components before jumping in. The China Index (quoted as CYX) traded on the Chicago Board Options Exchange (CBOE), for example, has a portfolio consisting of 20 Chinese stocks, many of which are among China's largest companies (see Table 8.2).

TABLE 8.2 STOCK COMPONENTS OF THE CBOE CHINA INDEX

Symbol	Company	Weight
ACH	Aluminum Corp. of China Ltd	5.00%
CEO	CNOOC Ltd	5.00%
CHA	China Telecom Corp. Ltd	5.00%
CHINA	Chinadotcom Corp.	5.00%
CHL	China Mobile Ltd	5.00%
CHU	China Unicom Ltd	5.00%
CN	China Netcom Group Corp. Hong	5.00%
CYD	China Yuchai International Ltd	5.00%
HNP	Huaneng Power International Inc.	5.00%
LFC	China Life Insurance	5.00%
NTE	Nam Tai Electronics Inc.	5.00%
NTES	Netease.com, Inc.	5.00%
PTR	PetroChina Co. Ltd	5.00%
SINA	Sina Corp.	5.00%
SMI	Semiconductor Manufacturing	5.00%
SNDA	Shanda Interactive Entertainment Ltd	5.00%
SNP	China Petroleum & Chemical Corp.	5.00%
SOHU	Sohu.com Inc.	5.00%
TOMO	TOM Online Inc.	5.00%
UTSE	Utstarcom Inc.	5.00%

Components as of June 17, 2005.
Source: Chicago Board Options Exchange.

In addition, there are several other indexes that provide the opportunity to invest in Asia stocks generally—the CBOE Asia 25 Index Options and the Hong Kong Option Index traded on NASDAQ, for example. It's worthwhile considering, though, that investing in so-called Asia indexes may not necessarily provide the opportunity to capitalize on China's growth, as some of these stocks have no businesses in China. The CBOE Asia 25 Index, for example, includes

25 stocks, and as of August 1, 2005, its portfolio did include nine Chinese stocks, but also companies from India, Indonesia, and South Korea. In this case, the index even includes stocks *not* from Asia—three Australian companies are in the index as well. So what can be marketed as an "Asia" index may not necessarily be the case.

PERFORMANCE OF LEADING COMPANIES

The year 2005 saw consumers not only in the United States but also around the world getting used to some fairly hefty hikes in the prices of oil and gas. It is not surprising, then, that two of China's top oil and gas companies were among the best performers on the China market over the past year or so. Among the companies in the China 25 Index (FXI25), three of them—PetroChina, CNOOC Ltd, and China Petroleum & Chemical—are oil and gas companies. Other big sectors were transport, construction, telecommunications, and energy companies (see Tables 8.3 and 8.4).

PUBLIC OFFERINGS OF CHINESE COMPANIES
IN THE UNITED STATES

Anyone watching the recent U.S. initial public offering (IPO) of Chinese search engine Baidu.com Inc. could have been excused for thinking time had transported them back to the height of the dot-com era in 2000. In fact, it's not too far from the truth, with investment firm Renaissance Capital estimating that the Baidu IPO on August 15, 2005, was the most successful since semiconductor and communications devices maker Marvell Technology's IPO in June 2000.

Many people may have noticed some similarities with the IPO of Google, which debuted on NASDAQ almost a year to the day earlier, on August 19, 2004. Shares of the Beijing-based

Baidu opened at $66, more than double its $27 offering price, and closed on the historic opening day at $122.54. While the price has since fallen, the immense interest the IPO attracted shows just how much potential the U.S. market believed there is in the Chinese market. One factor may have been that Baidu is 2.6 percent owned by Google. Although Baidu's market share does not compare with Google's, China's immense market of Internet users is likely to give it great potential over the longer run.

Baidu is one of several Chinese companies that have debuted on U.S. exchanges over the past couple of years. In fact, in 2005 there were six Chinese IPOs on the NASDAQ; the six companies raised $639 million. On the NYSE two companies—China Netcom Group Corp. Hong Kong Ltd and Suntech Power Holdings Co. Ltd—made their debuts. Both the NASDAQ companies and the NYSE companies have risen since, with the NASDAQ companies rising by 39 percent on average as of February 2006.

Tables 8.5 and 8.6 summarize the Chinese IPOs over this period and their performances.

PERFORMANCE OF MUTUAL FUNDS

Mutual funds have seen dramatic growth in the United States over the past two decades. At the beginning of the 1980s only a small percentage of Americans had investments in mutual funds, but both participation and total assets held in the funds have skyrocketed since then. Mostly this has been the result of increased participation in the stock market by individuals and the growth of employer-sponsored retirement plans.

The growth over the past quarter century has been extraordinary, as shown in Table 8.7. In 1980, just 5.7 percent of U.S. households (or 4.6 million households) held investments in a mutual fund, according to research by the Investment Company Institute and the U.S. Census Bureau estimates of the number of U.S.

TABLE 8.3 PERFORMANCE OF CHINESE COMPANIES LISTED ON THE NEW YORK STOCK EXCHANGE IN 2005

Company Name	China Region	Ticker	Listed Date	Sector	Close Price	As at Date	Close Price	As at Date	Rise/Fall	Rise/Fall %
PetroChina Co. Ltd	China	PTR	April 6, 2000	Oil & Gas	50.93	Dec. 31, 2004	81.96	Dec. 30, 2005	31.03	60.93%
Hutchison Telecommunications International Ltd	Hong Kong	HTX	Oct. 14, 2004	Telecommunications	13.55	Dec. 31, 2004	21.59	Dec. 30, 2005	8.04	59.34%
Tommy Hilfiger Corp.	Hong Kong	TOM	Sept. 22, 1992	Clothing & Accessories	11.28	Dec. 31, 2004	16.24	Dec. 30, 2005	4.96	43.97%
China Mobile Ltd	China	CHL	Oct. 22, 1997	Telecommunications	17.16	Dec. 31, 2004	24.04	Dec. 30, 2005	6.88	40.09%
Aluminum Corp. of China Ltd	China	ACH	Dec. 11, 2001	Mining	56.33	Dec. 31, 2004	76.34	Dec. 30, 2005	20.01	35.52%
China Life Insurance	China	LFC	Dec. 17, 2003	Insurance	26.44	Dec. 31, 2004	35.28	Dec. 30, 2005	8.84	33.43%
Advanced Semiconductor Engineering Inc.	Taiwan	ASX	Sept. 29, 2000	Semiconductors	3.4	Dec. 31, 2004	4.49	Dec. 30, 2005	1.09	32.06%
CNOOC Ltd	Hong Kong	CEO	Feb. 27, 2001	Oil & Gas	52.72	Dec. 31, 2004	67.97	Dec. 30, 2005	15.25	28.93%
Taiwan Semiconductor Manufacturing Co. Ltd	Taiwan	TSM	Oct. 8, 1997	Semiconductors	7.81	Dec. 31, 2004	9.91	Dec. 30, 2005	2.1	26.89%
China Petroleum & Chemical Corp.	China	SNP	Oct. 18, 2000	Oil & Gas	39.48	Dec. 31, 2004	49.6	Dec. 30, 2005	10.12	25.63%
Nam Tai Electronics Inc.	Hong Kong	NTE	Jan. 23, 2003	Consumer Electronics	18.22	Dec. 31, 2004	22.5	Dec. 30, 2005	4.28	23.49%
Au Optronics Corp.	Taiwan	AUO	May 23, 2002	Electronics	12.85	Dec. 31, 2004	15.01	Dec. 30, 2005	2.16	16.81%
Sinopec Shanghai Petrochemical Co. Ltd	China	SHI	July 26, 1993	Chemicals	34.89	Dec. 31, 2004	38	Dec. 30, 2005	3.11	8.91%

Company	Country	Symbol	IPO Date	Industry		Dec. 31, 2004		Dec. 30, 2005		
China Unicom Ltd	China	CHU	June 21, 2000	Telecommunications	7.73	Dec. 31, 2004	8.18	Dec. 30, 2005	0.45	5.82%
China Telecom Corp. Ltd	China	CHA	Nov. 14, 2002	Telecommunications	35.9	Dec. 31, 2004	36.58	Dec. 30, 2005	0.68	1.89%
PCCW Ltd	Hong Kong	PCW	Jan. 8, 2003	Telecommunications	6.03	Dec. 31, 2004	5.97	Dec. 30, 2005	-0.06	-1.00%
Chunghwa Telecom Co. Ltd	Taiwan	CHT	July 17, 2003	Telecommunications	19.57	Dec. 31, 2004	18.35	Dec. 30, 2005	-1.22	-6.23%
Asia Satellite Telecommunications Holdings Ltd	Hong Kong	SAT	June 18, 1996	Telecommunications	18.25	Dec. 31, 2004	16.95	Dec. 30, 2005	-1.3	-7.12%
Huaneng Power International Inc.	China	HNP	Oct. 6, 1994	Electric Utility	28.82	Dec. 31, 2004	26.21	Dec. 30, 2005	-2.61	-9.06%
United Microelectronics Corp.	Taiwan	UMC	Sept. 19, 2000	Semiconductors	3.52	Dec. 31, 2004	3.12	Dec. 30, 2005	-0.4	-11.36%
APT Satellite Holdings Ltd	Hong Kong	ATS	Dec. 17, 1996	Telecommunications	1.55	Dec. 31, 2004	1.3	Dec. 30, 2005	-0.25	-16.13%
Guangshen Railway Co. Ltd	China	GSH	May 13, 1996	Transportation	19.69	Dec. 31, 2004	15.52	Dec. 30, 2005	-4.17	-21.18%
Brilliance China Automotive Holdings Ltd	Hong Kong	CBA	Oct. 9, 1992	Auto Manufacturers	19.24	Dec. 31, 2004	14.59	Dec. 30, 2005	-4.65	-24.17%
Yanzhou Coal Mining Co. Ltd	China	YZC	March 31, 1998	Mining	43.44	Dec. 31, 2004	32.03	Dec. 30, 2005	-11.41	-26.27%
China Eastern Airlines Corp. Ltd	China	CEA	Feb. 4, 1997	Airlines	21.82	Dec. 31, 2004	15.61	Dec. 30, 2005	-6.21	-28.46%
China Southern Airlines Co. Ltd	China	ZNH	July 30, 1997	Airlines	19.86	Dec. 31, 2004	14.2	Dec. 30, 2005	-5.66	-28.50%
Semiconductor Manufacturing International Corp.	China	SMI	March 17, 2004	Semiconductors	10.77	Dec. 31, 2004	6.76	Dec. 30, 2005	-4.01	-37.23%
Global-Tech Appliances Inc.	Hong Kong	GAI	April 8, 1998	Durable Household	8.93	Dec. 31, 2004	3.76	Dec. 30, 2005	-5.17	-57.89%
									Average Rise/Fall	6.04%

Source: Mergent Analysis.

155

TABLE 8.4 PERFORMANCE OF CHINESE COMPANIES LISTED ON NASDAQ IN 2005

Company Name	Ticker	Listed Date	Region	Close Price	As at Date	Close Price	As at Date	Rise/ Fall	Rise/ Fall %
Shanda Interactive Entertainment Ltd	SNDA	May 12, 2004	Cayman Islands	42.5	Dec. 31, 2004	15.24	Dec. 30, 2005	−27.26	−64.14%
CtripCom International Ltd	CTRP	Sept. 12, 2003	Cayman Islands	45.75	Dec. 31, 2004	57.75	Dec. 30, 2005	12	26.23%
Netease.com, Inc.	NTES	June 30, 2000	Cayman Islands	52.92	Dec. 31, 2004	56.16	Dec. 30, 2005	3.24	6.12%
Sunday Communications Ltd	SDAY	March 15, 2000	Cayman Islands	5.46	Dec. 31, 2004	6.97	Dec. 30, 2005	1.51	27.66%
Siliconware Precision Industries Co.	SPIL	Sept. 7, 2000	Taiwan	3.71	Dec. 31, 2004	6.94	Dec. 30, 2005	3.23	87.06%
Radica Games Limited	RADA	April 13, 1994	Hong Kong	7.77	Dec. 31, 2004	8.91	Dec. 30, 2005	1.14	14.67%
TOM Online Inc.	TOMO	March 10, 2004	Cayman Islands	15.26	Dec. 31, 2004	19.82	Dec. 30, 2005	4.56	29.88%
Bonso Electronics International Inc.	BNSO	June 27, 1989	Hong Kong	5.2	Dec. 31, 2004	4.06	Dec. 30, 2005	−1.14	−21.92%
I-Cable Communications Ltd	ICAB	Nov. 24, 1999	Hong Kong	7.02	Dec. 31, 2004	4.6	Dec. 30, 2005	−2.42	−34.47%
Sina Corporation	SINA	April 13, 2000	Cayman Islands	32.06	Dec. 31, 2004	24.16	Dec. 30, 2005	−7.9	−24.64%
Peak International Limited	PEAK	June 20, 1997	Hong Kong	4.1	Dec. 31, 2004	2.66	Dec. 30, 2005	−1.44	−35.12%
Linktone Ltd	LTON	April 3, 2004	Cayman Islands	8.4	Dec. 31, 2004	10.38	Dec. 30, 2005	1.98	23.57%
China Natural Resources Inc.	CHNR	Aug. 7, 1995	British Virgin Islands	5.37	Dec. 31, 2004	3.66	Dec. 30, 2005	−1.71	−31.84%

Company	Ticker	IPO Date	Location	Price	Date	Price	Date	Change	%
Grand Toys International Inc.	GRIN	Aug. 17, 2004 (relisted)	Hong Kong	2.7	Dec. 31, 2004	1.5	Dec. 30, 2005	-1.2	-44.44%
Deswell Industries Inc.	DSWL	July 19, 1995	Hong Kong	15.72	Dec. 31, 2004	10.76	Dec. 30, 2005	-4.96	-31.55%
Highway Holdings Limited	HIHO	Nov. 12, 1996	Hong Kong	3.92	Dec. 31, 2004	3.18	Dec. 30, 2005	-0.74	-18.88%
City Telecom Ltd	CTEL	March 11, 1999	Hong Kong	3.95	Dec. 31, 2004	1.37	Dec. 30, 2005	-2.58	-65.32%
LJ International Inc.	JADE	April 17, 1998	Hong Kong	2.97	Dec. 31, 2004	3.43	Dec. 30, 2005	0.46	15.49%
Macronix International	MXICY	Sept. 5, 1996	Taiwan	2.18	Dec. 31, 2004	1.56	Dec. 30, 2005	-0.62	-28.44%
Qiao Xing Universal Telephone Inc.	XING	Feb. 19, 1999	British Virgin Islands	8.55	Dec. 31, 2004	7.4	Dec. 30, 2005	-1.15	-13.45%
ASAT Holdings Limited	ASTT	Nov. 7, 2000	Cayman Islands	1.32	Dec. 31, 2004	0.77	Dec. 30, 2005	-0.55	-41.67%
CDC Corporation	CHINA	July 13, 1999	Cayman Islands	4.61	Dec. 31, 2004	3.2	Dec. 30, 2005	-1.41	-30.59%
51job Inc.	JOBS	July 7, 2004	Cayman Islands	51.97	Dec. 31, 2004	14.7	Dec. 30, 2005	-37.27	-71.71%
Kongzhong Corp.	KONG	July 9, 2004	Cayman Islands	9.61	Dec. 31, 2004	12.5	Dec. 30, 2005	2.89	30.07%
China Finance Online Co. Ltd	JRJC	Oct. 15, 2004	Hong Kong	11.02	Dec. 31, 2004	6.56	Dec. 30, 2005	-4.46	-40.47%
eLong Inc.	LONG	Oct. 28, 2004	British Virgin Islands	18.65	Dec. 31, 2004	10.1	Dec. 30, 2005	-8.55	-45.84%
Ninetowns Digital World Trade Holdings Ltd	NINE	Dec. 3, 2004	China	10.75	Dec. 31, 2004	5.67	Dec. 30, 2005	-5.08	-47.26%
The9 Ltd	NCTY	Dec. 15, 2004	Cayman Islands	23.62	Dec. 31, 2004	15.29	Dec. 30, 2005	-8.33	-35.27%
								Average Rise/Fall	-16.65%

Source: Mergent Analysis.

Table 8.5 Performance of China IPOs on the NASDAQ, 2005

Company Name	Ticker	Listed Date	Amount of Offering	Close Price	As at Date	Close Price	As at Date	Rise/Fall	Rise/Fall %
Silicon Motion Technology Corporation	SIMO	June 30, 2005	$ 70,000,000	10.5	June 30, 2005	15.94	Feb. 17, 2006	5.44	51.81%
Focus Media Holding Limited	FMCN	July 13, 2005	$172,000,000	20.2	July 13, 2005	50.2	Feb. 17, 2006	30	148.51%
Baiducom Inc.	BIDU	Aug. 5, 2005	$109,000,000	122.54	Aug. 5, 2005	50.06	Feb. 17, 2006	−72.48	−59.15%
China Medical Technologies Inc.	CMED	Aug. 10, 2005	$ 75,000,000	16.2	Aug. 10, 2005	34.93	Feb. 17, 2006	18.73	115.62%
Hurray! Holding Co. Ltd	HRAY	Feb. 4, 2005	$ 71,000,000	10.25	Feb. 4, 2005	8.09	Feb. 17, 2006	−2.16	−21.07%
China Techfaith Wireless Communication Technology Ltd	CNTF	May 6, 2005	$142,000,000	15.32	May 6, 2005	15.83	Feb. 17, 2006	0.51	3.33%
							Average Rise/Fall		39.84%

Source: NASDAQ/Mergent Inc.

Table 8.6 Performance of China IPOs on the New York Stock Exchange, 2004 and 2005

Company Name	Ticker	Listed Date	Sector	Close Price	As at Date	Close Price	As at Date	Rise/Fall %
China Netcom Group Corp. Hong Kong Ltd	CN	Nov. 16, 2004	Telecommunications	24.81	Nov. 16, 2004	34.3	Feb. 16, 2006	38.25%
Suntech Power Holdings Co. Ltd	STP	Dec. 14, 2005	Electrical Components	21.2	Dec. 14, 2005	36.66	Feb. 16, 2006	72.92%

Source: Mergent Analysis.

TABLE 8.7 NUMBER OF LONG-TERM
MUTUAL FUNDS IN UNITED STATES,
1974 TO 2004

Year	Number of Funds
1974	431
1984	1,243
1994	5,325
2004	8,044

Source: Investment Company Institute.

households. By 1990, the percentage had risen to 25 percent (or 23.4 million households), and by 2000 it had nearly doubled again to 49 percent (or 51.7 million households). In 2001, 52 percent (or 56.3 million households) had investments in mutual funds.[1] At the end of 2004 there were more than 8,000 mutual funds in the United States, and together they held about $8.1 trillion in assets.[2]

The nature of investments held by mutual funds varies widely. Investment portfolios range from equities to bonds, and funds invest in different sectors, from biotechnology to property, and in different-sized companies. Funds also invest in various countries, with China being one of them. At the time of writing, there were approximately 30 funds for retail investors that specifically focus on China. The leading funds by net assets as of January 2006 included Fidelity China Region Fund (FHKCX), Matthews China (MCHFX), Guinness Atkinson China & Hong Kong (ICHKX), Templeton China World A (TCWAX), and Eaton Vance Greater China Growth A (EVCGX). Table 8.8 lists selected China-focused mutual funds in the United States, their performance data, and other fund details.

TABLE 8.8 **SELECTED CHINA-FOCUSED MUTUAL FUNDS AND PERFORMANCE DATA**

Fund Family	Fund	Ticker	As of
Templeton	Templeton China World A	TCWAX	Jan. 31, 2006
Templeton	Templeton China World C	TCWCX	Jan. 31, 2006
Fidelity	Fidelity China Region	FHKCX	Jan. 31, 2006
Eaton Vance	Eaton Vance Greater China Growth A	EVCGX	Jan. 31, 2006
Eaton Vance	Eaton Vance Greater China Growth B	EMCGX	July 31, 2005
Eaton Vance	Eaton Vance Greater China Growth C	ECCGX	July 31, 2005
Columbia Newport	Columbia Newport Greater China Z	LNGZX	July 31, 2005
Columbia Newport	Columbia Newport Greater China A	NGCAX	July 31, 2005
Columbia Newport	Columbia Newport Greater China C	NGCCX	July 31, 2005
Columbia Newport	Columbia Newport Greater China B	NGCBX	July 31, 2005
US Global Investors	China Region Opportunity Fund	USCOX	July 31, 2005
Guinness Atkinson	Guinness Atkinson China & Hong Kong	ICHKX	July 31, 2005
Alger	Alger China U.S. Growth Fund	CHUSX	July 31, 2005
AllianceBernstein	AllianceBernstein Great China '97 A	GCHAX	July 31, 2005
AllianceBernstein	AllianceBernstein Great China '97 C	GCHCX	July 31, 2005
AllianceBernstein	AllianceBernstein Great China '97 B	GCHBX	July 31, 2005
Gartmore	Gartmore China Opportunities A	GOPAX	July 31, 2005
Gartmore	Gartmore China Opportunities B	GOPBX	July 31, 2005
Gartmore	Gartmore China Opportunities C	GOPCX	July 31, 2005
Matthews	Matthews China	MCHFX	July 31, 2005
Dreyfus Premier	Dreyfus Premier Greater China R	DPCRX	July 31, 2005
Dreyfus Premier	Dreyfus Premier Greater China A	DPCAX	July 31, 2005
Dreyfus Premier	Dreyfus Premier Greater China T	DPCTX	July 31, 2005
Dreyfus Premier	Dreyfus Premier Greater China C	DPCCX	July 31, 2005
Dreyfus Premier	Dreyfus Premier Greater China B	DPCBX	July 31, 2005
			Average YTD Return

Source: Mergent Analysis.

YTD Return	5-Year Trailing Return	Yield	Minimum Initial Investment	Fund Inception Date
6.07%	N/A	1.30%	$1,000	Aug. 11, 2003
6.02%	N/A	0.99%	$1,000	Aug. 11, 2003
5.04%	7.04%	1.08%	$2,500	Nov. 1, 1995
7.99%	6.27%	0.70%	$1,000	Oct. 28, 1992
7.90%	5.57%	0.25%	$1,000	June 10, 1993
7.92%	5.52%	0.35%	$1,000	Dec. 28, 1993
11.96%	10.36%	1.77%	$1,000	May 16, 1997
11.95%	9.51%	1.62%	$1,000	May 16, 1997
11.86%	8.67%	0.98%	$1,000	May 16, 1997
11.86%	8.70%	1.00%	$1,000	May 16, 1997
10.62%	12.60%	2.27%	$5,000	Feb. 10, 1994
97.50%	6.42%	3.97%	$2,500	June 30, 1994
12.86%	N/A	N/A	$1,000	Nov. 3, 2003
13.10%	9.80%	0.43%	$2,500	Sept. 3, 1997
13.10%	8.99%	N/A	$2,500	Sept. 3, 1997
13.07%	9.06%	N/A	$2,500	Sept. 3, 1997
11.56%	N/A	0.62%	$2,000	June 29, 2004
11.45%	N/A	0.28%	$2,000	June 29, 2004
11.45%	N/A	0.26%	$2,000	June 29, 2004
10.91%	16.66%	1.33%	$2,500	Feb. 19, 1998
14.74%	10.84%	0.25%	$1,000	May 12, 1998
14.71%	10.50%	0.05%	$1,000	May 12, 1998
14.65%	10.52%	N/A	$1,000	March 1, 2000
14.62%	9.65%	N/A	$1,000	May 12, 1998
14.63%	9.62%	N/A	$1,000	May 12, 1998
14.70 %				

Even though many of the key Chinese stock indexes have trended downward over the past year, China-focused mutual funds in the United States have turned in strong performances overall, with more than half returning greater than 20 percent. In fact, an analysis of the 25 key mutual funds that focus on the China markets shows they averaged 14.7 percent in the year ended January 31, 2005.[3] This is good news for the investors who were on board over a year ago, with most funds outperforming many of the major U.S. stocks.

THE SOLE CHINA-FOCUSED EXCHANGE-TRADED FUND

At the time of writing, the only China stock–focused exchange-traded fund (ETF) anywhere in the world that focused on Chinese indexes was the FTSE/Xinhua China 25 Index Fund. Trading on the New York Stock Exchange and the NASDAQ under the ticker symbol FXI, the fund follows the FTSE/Xinhua China 25 Index, one of the China indexes to see the strongest growth over the past couple of years. The FTSE/Xinhua China 25 Index is one of the leading indexes of Chinese stocks and, as such, the fund's holdings include China Mobile (Hong Kong) Ltd, PetroChina Co. Ltd, BOC Hong Kong, CNOOC, and China Petroleum & Chemical Corp. (Sinopec)—among the largest and most liquid Chinese companies available to U.S. investors. Like most ETFs, although it follows an index, it may invest in some nonindex stocks from time to time for management reasons. In the case of the FTSE/Xinhua China 25 Index Fund, it plans to invest at least 90 percent of its assets in securities of the index, or in ADRs based on securities in the index. As of February 2006 the composition of the FTSE/Xinhua China 25 Index, and hence the fund itself, was mainly comprised of telecommunications, en-

TABLE 8.9 FTSE/XINHUA CHINA 25
INDEX FUND PORTFOLIO COMPOSITION
BY SECTOR

Sector	Composition %
Financials	24.69%
Oil & Gas	23.30%
Telecommunications	19.79%
Industrials	16.72%
Basic Materials	11.11%
Utilities	4.36%

Note: As of February 16, 2006.
Source: iShares.

ergy, and financial services stocks (see Table 8.9), which have been among the best performers over the past year.

The fund, however, is a new addition to the ETF market and, as such, presents an opportunity to invest in the top Chinese stocks via an ETF. It launched on the New York Stock Exchange on October 8, 2005, and has attracted much attention since its listing. A similar and related fund, also based on the China 25 Index, launched on the Hong Kong Stock Exchange in June 2005.

One of the reasons the FTSE/Xinhua China 25 Index has attracted attention is its performance: With a number of China's indexes falling over the past year, so, too, have the performances of many mutual funds that invest in Chinese stocks. In China, the mutual fund industry saw a loss of around US$741 million in the first half of 2005, according to official Chinese government figures,[4] following sluggish performance in the broader market. The FTSE/Xinhua China 25 Index, however, grew 20.30 percent in the year July 2004 to June 30, 2005.[5] Accordingly, so too has the FTSE/Xinhua China 25 Index Fund; it grew 33.41 percent from February 1, 2005, to February 1, 2006 (see Figure 8.3).

Stock Price in Dollars

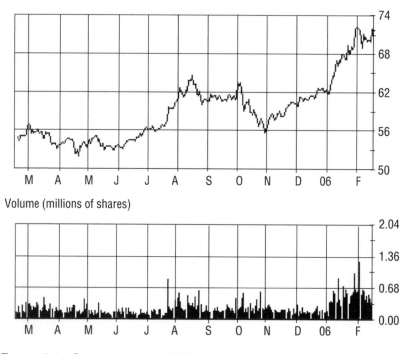

FIGURE 8.3 **PERFORMANCE OF FXI ON NEW YORK STOCK EXCHANGE, FEBRUARY 2005 TO FEBRUARY 2006**
Source: New York Stock Exchange.

The FTSE/Xinhua China 25 Index Fund was also in the top 12 percent of all ETFs traded in terms of year-to-date returns as of January 31, 2006[6] (see Table 8.10). It was also the best EFT after the South Korean ETF for the year ended January 31, 2006, among the 10 or so ETFs that focus on Asia or the Asia-Pacific region, growing 35.08 percent on a market return basis.

TABLE 8.10   PERFORMANCE OF FTSE/XINHUA CHINA 25 INDEX FUND VERSUS OTHER KEY ASIA AND ASIA-PACIFIC EXCHANGE-TRADED FUNDS

Fund Name	Ticker	YTD Return (Market)	One-Year Return (Market)	Three-Year Return (Market)
iShares FTSE/Xinhua China 25 Index Fund	FXI	16.44%	35.08%	N/A
iShares MSCI Australia Index	EWA	8.45%	25.55%	33.79%
iShares MSCI Taiwan Index	EWT	8.01%	15.68%	15.55%
iShares MSCI South Korea Index	EWY	7.73%	56.58%	40.72%
iShares MSCI Pacific ex-Japan	EPP	7.23%	22.32%	30.48%
iShares MSCI Singapore (Free) Index	EWS	6.58%	19.28%	30.74%
iShares MSCI Malaysia (Free) Index	EWM	6.45%	4.69%	14.06%
iShares MSCI Hong Kong Index	EWH	6.26%	19.64%	24.14%

All nonintraday data as of January 31, 2006.

CHAPTER 9

THE WORLD
OF TOMORROW

CHINA HAS been called a macroeconomic power. This is true in the sense that China's economy and market are exceptionally complex by western standards. The diversity within China serves both as an advantage in many respects and as a disadvantage in others.

In tracking China's economy since 1980, the emergence of China as a strengthening economic power is apparent, but it is not simply a matter of having more goods to export, or of selling more goods to the rest of the world. China's growth in output (measured by nominal dollar purchasing parity) increased from 3.2 percent of the world economic output in 1980 to 12.6 percent by 2003 (adjusted for price differences), placing China second only to the United States. During this quarter century, China passed Japan, Germany, France, the United Kingdom, Italy, and Russia, as shown in Figure 9.1.

Note what has occurred. All countries have lost output share except China. This is perhaps the most accurate long-term measurement because, based on the International Monetary Fund (IMF) data, China's growth has been consistent over the period. By 2004, China's economy had grown to be the world's seventh largest.[1] But when increased purchasing power in real dollars for China is factored in, and as the chart shows, China is, in fact, the second largest world economy today.

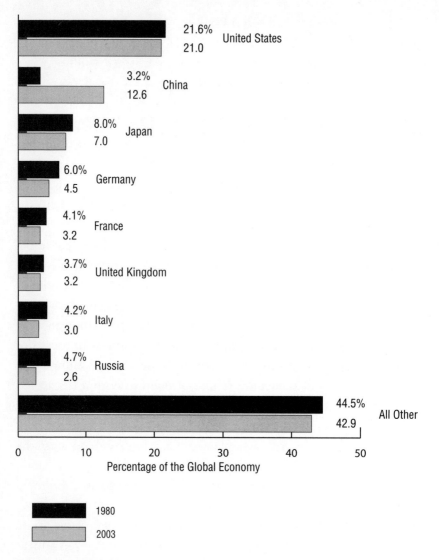

FIGURE 9.1 GLOBAL ECONOMY BY COUNTRY

Source: International Monetary Fund.

The growth has not been limited to output. China has also become the world's biggest recipient of foreign direct investment (FDI), having accumulated an aggregate total since 1980 of $501 billion.[2] These data naturally have been accompanied by relocations of business centers and the opening of China-based subsidiaries, notably in manufacturing. With its low production costs and cheap, efficient labor, China is expected to continue dominating world manufacturing until midcentury.

The competitive labor market represents a huge problem for so many countries outside China. Even given the impediments to continued growth economically (most notably, related to energy consumption as discussed previously), many foreign manufacturers are running scared today. As the lead to a 2004 cover story in one U.S. magazine warned in relation to competition from China, "Cut your price at least 30 percent or lose your customers."[3]

There are problems in China, as well, of course. Over the past 15 years, China has doubled its electricity consumption, with more demand expected in the future.[4] Overall, Chinese demand for raw materials and energy equaled one-fifth of worldwide demand in metals.[5] Increases in energy usage, metals, petroleum, and raw materials present a problem in many respects. The demand drives up world prices and may also be difficult, if not impossible, to meet in the future. In other words, China's growth cannot continue without constraints, for practical reasons. Limited supplies of petroleum, metals, other raw materials, and even coal would eventually prevent China from enjoying ever-increasing growth rates. The need for alternative, more efficient, and cleaner fuel sources is immediate, but the Chinese manufacturing base requires raw materials as well, and this may present a chronic problem, not only in China but throughout the world.

China has additional demographic problems. Massive numbers of people are leaving rural China and migrating to the urban centers searching for better-paying jobs. In spite of crowding, high unemployment, and pollution concerns, the migration continues. It is a problem similar to that experienced in the early eighteenth century in England. During the height of the Industrial Revolution, dozens of towns and smaller cities were emptied out, sometimes completely, as people migrated to the large manufacturing cities to get high-paying jobs working machines. Today in China, a similar influx of people to the cities is creating a problem for the same reasons—not so much the loss of agricultural production, but more because of the problem of managing large numbers of untrained, unskilled people all seeking jobs in a finite market.

Finally, China faces substantial problems in trying to shore up its financial markets. The Chinese banking system, often described as fragile or, at best, uncertain, could be the Achilles' heel in the rapid growth plan and capitalization of Chinese infrastructure. Given the transition from state-controlled to free-market banking and finance, accompanied by the notorious historical record of corruption and exaggerated earnings, the financial sector in China requires more reform than most other sectors. At the same time, it is so essential to continuing the development of industrial China at its current rate. Direct foreign investment has grown at the incredible rate of 50 percent over five years from 1999 to 2004; and all other economic signs have moved upward at the same pace. However, continued growth rests on the premise that the growth curve can continue to be capitalized effectively.[6]

Growth rates have been impressive, but many problems will limit the continuation and expansion of that growth. These include finite supplies of energy and raw materials, demographic problems within industrialized and urban China, continuing unemployment, and the slow pace of training for higher-paying skilled jobs in technology and other fields.

THE EMERGING CHINESE CONSUMER

In the past, the Chinese consumer was viewed as a nonfactor in the Chinese economy. With little or no disposable income, ordinary

Chinese families were seen by those outside of China as being in no position to have any impact on either domestic or international markets. That view remains widely held today outside China, but it is inaccurate.

Today, China's middle class is growing and expanding at a greater rate than has ever before been the case in the country's history. In 1980, per capita GDP was $411, and by 2003 it had grown to $4,900.[7] As this change has occurred, so has domestic consumption within China. By 2010, estimates are that Chinese consumers will hold 22 percent of all televisions in the world, 12 percent of personal computers, and 11 percent of automobiles. These statistics in 1990 were 12 percent (televisions), and 1 percent each in computer and automobile ownership.[8]

As the Chinese family's income grows, so does consumption. This economic success is not limited to the growing middle classes. In the very near future, according to estimates, China will have more millionaires (est. 236,000) than Canada (200,000 millionaires).[9] The emerging Chinese middle class, at 130 million people, is larger than the entire combined population of the United Kingdom and France.[10]

Those outside China may view these emerging economic and demographic trends as merely interesting but having little if any impact elsewhere in the world. This is a mistake. For investors, the future value of investment decisions made today will be determined by trends such as these. Increased demand for raw materials and the need for new fuel efficiency and alternative fuel sources—and the resulting impact of prices in all metals and raw materials—provide a clue about how and where investments are going to pay off. The Chinese consumer is also becoming a major purchaser in dozens of other areas: telecommunications, electronics, computers, industrial machinery, automobiles, and appliances. China already purchases more television sets than the United States, a reality that only a few years ago was unimaginable. China is now the largest market for consumer products overall. In the past the United States, Japan, and Europe were the focus of manufacturers.

It is especially interesting that foreign direct investment in China originated as a means for taking advantage of low labor costs and basing plants in China for exporting activity. Today, those same firms often are addressing Chinese demand at an ever-increasing rate, another hint about where consumption may be centered in the future. By 2004, for example, U.S.-based auto manufacturers (as well as auto corporations in other countries) were committing more than $12 billion per year to develop manufacturing plants in China, with this level being fed by a growing domestic demand for both passenger and commercial automobiles.[11] In fact, by 2010, China is expected to represent 35 percent of global demand for heavy trucks alone.[12]

Industrialized nations have long viewed China as a potentially lucrative market. However, this point of view has usually been based on the idea that China's large population represents new customers. This is partially true and as the Chinese consumer's per capita income grows, so will demand for both domestically and for-eign-made goods. However, it is more debatable to identify who is likely to benefit the most from China's growth, China itself or other countries.

China has an advantage in its growth curve, in the sense that foreign interests have invested (and continue to invest) heavily in China's industry and markets. This global belief in China's growth—which funds the growth itself—is also a strong funda-mental sign for investors that the current rate of growth is not a passing fad. China is going to dominate markets in the future at an accelerating pace. Companies whose research and involvement are directly in the China markets, notably Xinhua Finance, will in-evitably play dominant roles in providing product and service sup-port to a growing investor base as well.

The most popular indicator that foreign analysts point to is cheap labor. This is certainly a factor that will enable China to con-tinue competing successfully with foreign manufacturing centers, but it is not the only factor. China is not entirely vulnerable to labor markets, because its advantage is multifaceted. Industry continues to receive government patronage at varying levels, which further helps those industries compete internationally. And because low fixed investment costs allow China to continue its own infrastructural development, real growth can occur more rapidly in China than in most other industrialized nations and regions.

A global partnership is inevitable, and investors need to be aware of this interaction. Combining China's low costs and affordable labor with overseas financial investment and technological skills, China has a distinct competitive advantage that involves manufacturing industries, but much more as well.

Another factor indicating a Chinese advantage, but one not well known outside China, is the extensive internal distribution network that Chinese corporations have developed. Consumer product companies in China have constructed systems with thousands of outlets, not only throughout the provinces and large cities, but in smaller cities as well. The long-standing and strong relationships existing between firms and retail outlets make it difficult for outside corporations to compete. There is a tendency for foreign-based companies to define a global strategy in terms of identifying China-based investment in U.S. instruments or as simply the idea of opening up outlets in other countries. Thus, investors might be drawn to retailers like Wal-Mart that have established subsidiary operations throughout the world, including China. However, the mere presence of outlets does not ensure market domination as it may at home. Wal-Mart's U.S. success has been the result of a simple formula: lower prices, big volume in huge stores, a nonunion workforce, strong influence over its suppliers, and domination over its competitors. This may work to a degree in China, but even Wal-Mart will be competing there with other, previously established concerns that already have an existing relationship. Furthermore, a more subtle reality that may not show up in the numbers is a cultural aspect, the preference among Chinese outlets to work with and to trust domestic name brands over foreign name brands.

Everyone should keep in mind the fact that for the 30 years from 1949 to 1979, the Chinese consumer was not exposed to foreign brands at all. Even in postreform-era China, the domestic consumer has not automatically taken to foreign brands and Chinese manufacturers have the advantage of long-established name brand recognition and trust among its consumers.

A related point, also often overlooked by foreign investors, is that tastes and buying preferences are not universal within China. It is a complex society with a melded culture, and local manufacturers are aware of these subtle differences. There is a tendency among foreign competitors to assume that consumers are identical everywhere, so everyone will like Pepsi or a Big Mac equally well. That is far from automatic, and foreign companies need to research the Chinese market as a series of varying tastes and cultural preferences. For investors, the key to identifying potentially profitable long-term investments is to consider these variables as well.

FOREIGN COMPETITION: A REALISTIC VIEW

A related foreign view has long been that remnants of a communist mind-set are disadvantageous to China, and that free-market forces would be able to compete successfully with a country in which government intervention has been recognized for many years. Again, this is a mistake. The Chinese government is effectively managing its transition from state-controlled economic practice to a free-market economy. Even with the slow pace of movement away from state-owned enterprises (SOEs) and management of its high nonperforming loan problems (and handling of unemployed prior SOE workers), it would be a mistake to assume that Chinese companies cannot compete with long-established free-market competitors. The traditional trade barriers, such as prohibitive import tariffs, remain in some industries, but these are disappearing rapidly as a part of China's membership in the World Trade Organization (WTO). This may be the most significant economic change of all, one that may speed up domestic reform and changes in internal mind-sets within China. These changes will be seen in manufacturing, retail, and service sectors, as well as in liberalization and expansion of China's stock markets.

As import tariffs are disappearing rapidly, they are at times replaced with varying tax policies and outright subsidies, which, effectively, end up working in the same way as foreign tax incentive programs, such as tax credits for certain types of construction or employment or certain industries. More and more, internal practices that provide unfair advantage or favor domestic corporations are being rapidly phased out and eliminated. China wants and needs WTO participation, and it is cooperating in every way it needs to in order to ensure full membership.

Investors looking for specific growth industries *within* the Chinese economy may want to pay special attention to energy sectors, short-term infrastructure, and long-term technology. Domestic firms have developed local technological standards competing with and even surpassing foreign levels. For example, digital/audio networking, high-definition TV, chip technology, mobile transmission, and wireless industries have developed Chinese standards far ahead of western technology. Many standards will be under development for several years to come; others, like Enhanced Video Disc (EVD) technology, were in production as of 2004. The rapid development of these high-level advances and, often, of new global standards presents the possibility that in the near future, Chinese-based technology manufacturing may dominate world markets.[13]

Because many of these advances have not been explored outside China, the domestic technological manufacturers have a market advantage. Foreign competitors are far behind in many instances, a point that should not be lost on investors looking for companies offering a future competitive advantage. Regarding experience and market exposure of the past among foreign competitors, Chinese manufacturers are rapidly closing that competitive gap. In some cases, such as the new generation of EVD technology, the competitive advantage is even greater than the simple ability to penetrate existing markets. With foreign technology, China has to make royalty payments on all sales; however, with its own technology, those royalties are no longer required, which reduces the wholesale price as much as 13 percent on EVD formats.[14]

The same market advantage may well apply to TD-SCDMA (time division–synchronous code division multiple access), third-generation mobile phone standards not used outside China. If this becomes a universal standard, Chinese manufacturers may no longer pay royalty fees to foreign rights owners, *and* related development of network equipment and handsets may further improve China's international competitiveness. For foreign concerns, the competitive threat is twofold: direct sales through retail outlets are likely to suffer, and patent owners stand to lose royalty income. This double threat is part of the incentive behind China's ongoing development of next-generation technology in these technology industries. For investors, the trend is promising as well, as Chinese technology companies become more able to compete.

A potential downside should be kept in mind as well. China continues to depend on a limited internal supply of well-trained technology employees and has been slow to develop extensive but desperately needed training programs. This factor may inhibit China's ability to take full advantage of its own new technology in the future.

The labor problem itself has two conflicting aspects. The lack of high-tech skill and accompanying training programs may be a future inhibiting factor in creating and maintaining a competitive edge in technology. At the same time, high unemployment in less-skilled workers and a large labor pool to draw from keeps less-skilled labor expenses down. For example, U.S. automakers earn an average of $52.65 per hour; in China, the same jobs pay $1.25.[15]

The labor problem is not unique to China. Other Asian countries also pay very low wages, but lack China's accompanying high productivity. Even so, the cheap labor pool reflects an exceptionally high unemployment rate, which is made worse by the large-scale rural-to-urban migration among unskilled workers. Although China's official unemployment figure is similar to statistics in the United States—reported at 4.3 percent[16]—the *real* number has to include underemployment in rural areas. The national unemployment rate is realistically estimated closer to 21 percent.[17] A potentially inhibiting factor to unlimited growth in China's future is its need to create 12 million *new* jobs every year for the next decade just to keep up with new people entering its domestic labor market.[18] So on the one hand, continuing cheap labor is virtually ensured for China's manufacturers for the indefinite future, making it highly competitive with markets where labor has greater leverage; but, on the other hand, this apparent competitive advantage is not reserved exclusively for China-based manufacturers. Investors may be wise to remember that the same labor pool is available to foreign-owned and foreign-based manufacturers opening plants in China. So on a global scale, the large and cheap labor market within China could end up providing no long-term advantage to China-based companies. It could be a disadvantage, given foreign company markets and other capitalization-based and market advantages. This reality explains, at least in part, the rationale behind the growing FDI in China in the past quarter century. For example, the reported figures comparing autoworker pay per hour between U.S. workers (at $52.65 per hour) and Chinese workers (at $1.25 per hour) does not include manufacturing performed by domestic workers on behalf of foreign companies. Thus, the competitive advantage of China-based low labor costs helps *all* auto manufacturers making use of that market. It is a mistake to limit comparisons on the assumption that manufacturing is taking place in a domicile country exclusively. Increasingly, this is not the case. That low labor cost benefits all participants in the sector, domestic and foreign.

THE LAGGING TRAINING AND R&D PROBLEM

Any observer of the changes in China since 1979 has to admire the scope and extent of reforms and improvements made in the country. Numerous challenges remain, but it is clear that the Chinese government and industry have embraced the free market, and are excelling within it.

Perhaps the greatest internal problems remain high real unemployment among former SOE employees and untrained rural migrants. Although 250 million people work in the cities, another 490 million remain in rural Chinese areas.[19] City workers average 60 cents per hour, low by western standards but high in comparison to the typical rural worker's earnings of 20 cents per hour on average.[20] China has been slow to invest in training programs, even though it suffers the duality of high unskilled worker unemployment along with high demand for *skilled* worker jobs. Equally disturbing is the low investment by China and its domestic corporations in research and development (R&D). It invested only about 0.6 percent of GDP in 2002, compared to 3.1 percent invested by Japan, 2.6 percent each by both Korea and the United States, 2.5 percent by Germany, and 1.9 percent by the United Kingdom.[21]

The low investment in R&D is a distinct disadvantage for Chinese companies, but it is understandable in a historical context. After decades of becoming accustomed to state-controlled central planning, the concept of corporate-based R&D is a new idea. In fact, competition itself, which requires investment in R&D, is a new idea for many long-established Chinese firms. The problems of lack of training of workers and low investment in R&D are more political than cultural, and in the rapidly emerging free markets of China this lack of R&D funding is likely to disappear. Once the competitive value of R&D becomes apparent, it is likely that Chinese companies will embrace it. For investors, companies showing exceptional foresight by investing in R&D more aggressively than their competitors may also gain a distinct market advantage, which may translate into years' worth of competitive edge. What is needed may be a balance between gradual growth in per capita earnings and gradual improvement in the relative R&D and training-investment picture. Remember, too, that, even with the low comparative investment levels, Chinese firms did increase their total R&D investment by 400 percent between 1991 and 2002.[22] So although the level remains lower than in other industrialized nations, China is making progress.

For investors interested in spotting the next China investment opportunity (or series of opportunities), the field is broad. A key element is to view the various relative economic factors realistically, while also trying to understand the impact of emerging Chinese trends, not just within China but in foreign companies as well. The many industries, their global advantages or vulnerabilities, and likely changes in the future are all going to be affected by many emerging trends outside China, as well as within. The complexities of anticipating where these changes lead will vary, also, with a multitude of influencing factors: political change; rate of reform within China; energy shortages; cost and availability of fuel and raw materials; developments in the Middle East, North Korea, and other trouble spots; internal employment trends and migration; training and R&D investment; monetary exchange rates domestically and overseas; foreign investment; and, as much as anything else, trends within Chinese and global investment markets.

CHAPTER 10

RESEARCH IN THE NEW GLOBAL INVESTMENT ENVIRONMENT

PREDICTING FUTURE MARKET TRENDS

Apart from the short-term regulatory environment and the challenges faced by the Chinese government, which so far have been met largely with skill and great wisdom, the impact of Internet technology and its resultant effects as it expands in market applications will add to the ever-growing expansion of the China stock markets as they approach an efficient, global level. Due to the advantages of being a relatively new market, with new systems and modern regulation, the China markets have a potential advantage over the more established markets and firms in Wall Street, London, and elsewhere. It is reasonable to predict therefore that within a few years several significant changes could occur:

First, the international securities markets will become more fully global. The trend is already establishing itself, and this change is inevitable. Current trade barriers and restrictions on transfers of currency and the opening of accounts in foreign countries are becoming nonissues in several respects. Trading once unique to a particular country or market is now becoming multi-exchange in nature. China stocks can now be traded on the New York Stock Exchange in many cases, for example. The expansion of mutual funds, ETFs, and index-based funds and derivatives investing is breaking down barriers. The global market is already here—all that really remains is sorting out the details; settlement and custody of stock remain a challenge, but the force of the market is driving the solution.

Second, the traditional securities firms and information providers will find their dominance challenged in this new market. Today, many of the well-establish firms sit comfortably atop the market, some with a complete lack of awareness of the changes going on around them. For consumers, from the private investor to major investment houses, the problem is self-evident. Anyone trying to get information from a customer service line in any of the multifaceted "800-pound gorillas" knows this already. These companies are so expansive, so entrenched in all of the securities, news, and information markets, that they are becoming out of touch with their markets and unaware of the growing distrust of them. They predominate in U.S. equity and debt markets in particular, although this is also true in Europe, Australasia, and elsewhere. Much of the major stock trading among institutions (which represents the majority of all market activity), mutual funds, insurance, index providers, news, settlement, events data, and financial consultation is controlled by multibillion-dollar conglomerates. For the astute investor seeking objective, exceptional data and advice, the dominant consolidated firms are failing to deliver the crucial difference required to make good investment decisions. In this situation, dominance of the market is not enough. In fact, as the market goes global, these same firms are attempting to present a global strategy for investors, but they are poorly equipped to compete with local expertise, particularly in China where China-specific indexes, local ratings analysis, news, and databases of investment intelligence provide a true picture of the landscape. In the new environment, the large firms will not be able to compete on a global scale. They are increasingly providing poor service domestically (ironically, in some cases, as a result of outsourcing data collection and service centers to Asian markets!), and they appear unable to fix their domestic problems. So, you may properly ask, "How do these same firms expect to compete internationally, particularly in the new markets?"

Third, China-based exchanges will become major players in the global exchange market. With the advantage of new technologies and new markets yet with significant market size, the Chinese exchanges and the local added-value vendors are performing at a higher level of service than their equivalents in other long-established markets. Their market is currently tiny compared to current U.S. securities markets, for example, but the program is coming together rapidly throughout Asia, centered in Hong Kong, Shenzhen, and Shanghai, as well as in other Chinese financial and economic centers. The Chinese business community has embraced the free market and is thriving on it. The Chinese consumer is increasingly looking toward the benefits the free market offers, including the rewards of labor: houses, cars, appliances, electronics, savings, ever-expanding lifestyles, and personal security. The Chinese exchanges in conjunction with the authorities continue to work to reform their own system, including fixing problems of past corruption, valuation uncertainty, and inconsistencies in accounting standards. The advent of international accounting standards and audit practice, as well as the introduction of transparency and reporting standards, particularly XBRL (eXtensible Business Reporting Language) provides China with the opportunity to leap ahead of the rest of the world in this respect as the more established markets deal with the change and try to catch up. At the same time, in the U.S. markets the demands created by Sarbanes-Oxley legislation are creating heavy administrative and cost burdens to listed companies and are a major disincentive to those considering an initial public offering. This gives immediate competitive advantages to foreign stocks such as those in China.

Fourth, as part of an expanding and global competitive market, shares of Chinese companies will become even more available to the global market, not just to domestic investors. A part of China's emerging global business impact will be the inevitable expansion of its internal securities market. Today, various restrictions on who can own specific classifications of stock in Chinese companies are keeping the Chinese markets relatively small. However, ever-expanding interest in China's business community and its securities market will have another inevitable benefit: a change in the cultural limitation of most of China's securities market to domestic investors. We already know that there are ways around these direct ownership restrictions. By owning index fund shares, mutual funds, and ETFs, and by using derivatives for China-based indexes, virtually anyone can acquire a de facto equity position in China. As this reality becomes obvious to all, and as the benefits of an expanding equity and debt capitalization source continue to appeal to the Chinese business community and government, these foreign investment restrictions will disappear.

Fifth, the value of international research expertise will climb significantly. Given the virtual certainty of the expansion of Chinese markets impacting global markets and the resultant rebalancing in the size of the traditional markets, important related trends will take place as well, with China being a major driver of many of these changes. Currently, a large part of Wall Street's marketing is centered on the appeal to investors of expert financial research and advice. Moves have already been made by the authorities to bring more transparency and fairness to this research, and this will be reinforced as markets become more global and firms become able to offer (1) locally based research; (2) effective international trading capability through the Internet and similar low-cost means; (3) customer response from the local market rather than a centralized remote center; (4) global database information sources developed and updated by experts with local expertise; and (5) a truly global presence on many tiers, including research, product, and service lines; news; local and global indexes; and customer-response centers.

THE EVOLVING RESEARCH ENVIRONMENT

As the global market expands and changes around you, the importance and necessity of research will become increasingly crucial to your investment decisions. This is unavoidable.

The virtually global access to the Internet has changed everyone's lives in the same way that prior innovations have. The impacts of the telegraph, ticker tape, and telephone on U.S. stock markets in the nineteenth century were far-reaching. In the twentieth century, the automobile and air travel affected every segment of society. Even so, the potential of the Internet for investors was not even imagined until recently.

Today, investors—even those with only a small amount of capital—can easily plug directly into worldwide exchanges; buy and sell stock and other products; and find free news, quotes, charts, and other relevant information. Con artists, too, have the same access. It is essential today that everyone treats the information available online with caution and a healthy degree of skepticism. A good rule of thumb: Don't depend on "pushed information." You should ideally go to the source and generate information in response to questions you ask, with those answers derived from authoritative and legitimate online sources. If you depend on what you hear in investment chat rooms (where you have no idea who is there or what their motives are), you will not be able to rely on the information you gain. The only way to ensure that your data is of high quality, dependable, and based on research and valid secondary sources is to rely on companies with the resources you need. It is therefore worthwhile identifying who the accredited data providers, brokers, and exchanges are for each of the markets in which you are interested. If you plan to perform research based on yesterday's investment culture, you are already out of date. The blunt reality shows that, realistically, you can no longer rely on the research departments of older, established sources that are unable to adapt quickly enough to an increasingly fast moving and global market. Equally, while useful as a first reference tool, and for slightly delayed indicative market information, the typical Internet search engine or news tool is not a good source for research data.

A surprising amount of valuable information on Chinese markets and instruments is available today from accredited sources as discussed elsewhere. For the future China is already in the forefront of major developments that will make the average investor's life easier and in some cases is ahead of more established markets simply by virtue of being a relatively new player. A major example is the advent of XBRL, which will allow the researcher and investor alike to easily compare stocks, not only within their own markets, but also across international boundaries—and for the first time with transparency (i.e., the ability to quickly and easily discover how any ratio, estimate, or fundamental data item was derived and to review its source in a consistent manner across international boundaries). XBRL is a good example of future change as a language for the electronic communication of financial data, and it is set to affect business reporting around the world. It provides major benefits in the preparation, analysis, and communication of business information. It offers cost savings, greater efficiency, and improved accuracy and reliability to all those involved in supplying or using financial data. So the creators of the data, the companies themselves, and their auditors and advisers are motivated to produce data utilizing this standard, enabling the analyst or investor to make judgments much more easily than today.

XBRL is being developed by an international nonprofit consortium of approximately 250 major companies, organizations, and government agencies. In China the major player in promoting the use of XBRL is Xinhua Finance. It is an open standard, free of license fees. It is already being put to practical use in a number of countries, and implementations of XBRL are growing rapidly around the world.

INFORMATION SOURCES AND RESEARCH TOOLS

VALUABLE INFORMATION can be found using many sources. As complex as China is as an emerging world power, information for would-be investors is not difficult to locate. As is the case with any research source, quality varies, so you need to consider carefully the value of information from your sources before making investment decisions based on what you read.

Free services are valuable, to a degree. They may either provide starting points to follow news and trends or enable you to find out about the fundamentals of companies you are already interested in tracking. However, free services are usually supported by advertisers or companies with particular products or services to promote. Thus they may promote their own products and not others (but not necessarily). Such sources may also not always provide warnings about particular types of investments. So while free services are a good foundation for information, you may also need to pay for a reliable service for more detailed analysis. Subscription services may sometimes be more valuable because it is the paying consumer to whom they answer at the end of the day. Also consider where a source is located. If it is located in the United States it is subject to U.S. laws, such as those that relate to consumer protection, fair trading, privacy and data collection, product disclosure, and investment advisory laws. If a source is located in a country with a poor track record of requiring information providers to act fairly and honestly, then there may be greater risks that the information you consume is not as reliable as it could be. Numerous information services and web sites provide information on the Chinese market and, more specifically, investing in China. Some of these are government sanctioned, owned, or regulated (e.g., the Hong Kong Stock Exchange) and others are privately run. Whatever the case, you should always consider the reliability of information.

The following are some key information sources that provide detailed and generally reliable information on Chinese stocks (although we cannot testify to the reliability of particular aspects of information).

CHINESE STOCK EXCHANGES

Hong Kong Stock Exchange (HKSE)

Investors looking for information about investing in China can start with a basic study of the stock exchanges themselves. Found at www.hkex.com.hk, the HKSE site includes not only company fundamental data, earnings reports, other prices, and charts, but also information on the exchange's rules for listed companies, how the market is regulated and supervised, and how trades are conducted. The site is also a good starting point for investors wanting information on any of the Chinese stock exchanges. As previously explained, the regulatory environment and accounting standards for Hong Kong–listed stocks are most similar to western standards, whereas other bourses in China are less certain, and questions remain about whether value and earnings reports are reliable outside of the HKSE-listed stocks. Nevertheless, this site also includes numerous links to other valuable information sources, including details of and links to listed companies. It also provides online trading services and investor education. Another link on the site is to available equity, debt, and derivative products that can be traded on the exchange. These include stocks; warrants; pooled investments (mutual funds, ETFs, and unit investment trusts); bonds; and index products.

Hong Kong Growth Enterprise Market (GEM)

Another market linked to the Hong Kong Stock Exchange is the Growth Enterprise Market (GEM), the exchange where newer technology companies tend to be listed. The exchange is operated by Hong Kong Exchanges and Clearing Limited and can be accessed directly from the HKSE web site, or found at www.hkgem.com. The GEM differs from the main market in an important respect: It does not require companies to have the same record of profitability as a condition of listing on the HKSE requires. Thus it tends to attract new companies looking for early stage capital to grow. It is an incubator for Chinese venture-backed and private equity–backed companies. Numerous technology, Internet, communications, and biotech companies are listed on the GEM. Like the HKSE web site, the GEM web site carries data on publicly listed companies, market statistics, company announcements, details of new listings and upcoming IPOs, basic financial information on listed companies, and listing rules.

Shanghai and Shenzhen Stock Exchanges

The Shanghai Stock Exchange web site (www.sgx.com) and the Shenzhen Stock Exchange (www.szse.cn/main/en/) provide specific information about companies listed on these two exchanges. Some Chinese companies may be listed on the Hong Kong as well as the Shanghai or Shenzhen exchanges, but some are listed on just Shanghai or Shenzhen. These two exchanges have different listing requirements than the Hong Kong exchange. Their respective web sites similarly carry information relating to listed companies, listing requirements, trading rules, disclosures, listed company announcements, quotes and charts, and regulatory rules and regulations.

CHINESE REGULATORY AUTHORITIES

A number of sources are good starting points in the search by individual investors wanting to be more familiar with the operations of not only the Chinese stock markets and financial services industry, but regulation of the markets themselves.

China Banking Regulatory Commission

This commission, operated by the government, is responsible for supervising the banking and financial industry. It consists of 15 departments, and its functions are to regulate the industry, outline new laws and administrative regulations, approve and issue banking licenses, supervise banks and issue fines, oversee the qualifications of professionals, compile and publish statistics, and manage supervisory boards. Its web site publishes comprehensive statistics and a range of news and information (www.cbrc.gov.cn/english/).

Securities and Futures Commission

In Hong Kong, investment advisers are licensed and supervised by the Securities and Futures Commission. Its web site is a good potential source for additional research into general markets in China, and provides a "public register of licensed persons and registered institutions" where you can search by name or by regulated activity, review requirements for professionals, or contact the commission for additional information (www.hksfc.org.hk).

NOTES

INTRODUCTION   The New Face of World Economics

1. You Nuo, "Nation Hungry for Skilled Workers," *China Daily*, May 6, 2005.

CHAPTER 1   An Economic History of China

1. National Bureau of Statistics of China.
2. World Bank, "World Development Indicators," www.worldbank .org.
3. Fareed Zakaria, "Does the Future Belong to China?," *Newsweek*, May 9, 2005.
4. "Blackout Costs N.Y. City $1 Billion," Reuters, August 18, 2003.
5. Hannah Beech, "China's Long, Dark Summer," *Time Asia Magazine*, July 5, 2004.
6. Jay Apt and Lester B. Lave, "US: Blackouts Are Inevitable, Coping, Not Prevention, Should Be the Primary Goal," *Washington Post*, August 10, 2004.
7. George W. Bush, remarks at the Small Business Administration National Small Business Week Conference (Expo 2005), Washington, DC, April 27, 2005.
8. Jonathan Watts, "China's Growth Flickers to a Halt," *The Guardian*, July 4, 2004.
9. John Dizzard, "Bush, Iraq and the Hydrogen Economy," *Financial Times*, February 1, 2005.
10. *World Energy Outlook*, October 26, 2004.

11. William H. McNeill, *Plagues and People* (New York: Anchor Books, 1976).
12. Kenneth Pommerantz, *The Great Divergence: China, Europe, and the Making of the Modern World Economy* (Princeton, NJ: Princeton University Press, 2001).
13. Benjamin Elman, Professor of Chinese History, Princeton University.
14. Pamela C. M. Mar and Frank-Jürgen Richter, *China: Enabling a New Era of Changes* (Singapore: John Wiley & Sons [Asia], 2003).

CHAPTER 2   Worldwide Change and the Globalization of Investments

1. Benjamin Disraeli, speech, October 29, 1867.
2. Marco Polo, *Travels*, c. 1295. Reissue edition: *The Travels of Marco Polo* (London: Penguin Classics, 1958).
3. The first mutual fund, formed in 1924, was the Massachusetts Investors Trust. Within one year, it had grown from initial deposits of $50,000 to $392,000 and 200 shareholders. Today, over 10,000 funds exist with assets of $7 trillion and with 83 million individual shareholders. (*Source:* Investment Company Institute, www.ici.org; accessed September 2005.)
4. Marc Faber, *Tomorrow's Gold* (Hong Kong: CLSA Books, 2003).
5. *CIA World Factbook* and the U.S. Census Bureau.
6. "Mark Twain as Seen by His Housemaid," *New York Times*, March 15, 1925, www.twainquotes.com/91250315.html.
7. Dr. Eber Jeffery, *Journal of the Patent Office Society*, July 1940.
8. *Far Eastern Economic Review*, November 16, 1995.
9. Fareed Zakaria, "Does the Future Belong to China?," *Newsweek*, May 9, 2005.
10. "Beijing Forms Software Alliance to Beef Up Industry," China Online, December 21, 2001, www.chinaonline.com.

11. Fan Gang, "Reform and Development: The Dual-Transformation of China," in Pamela C. M. Mar and Frank-Jürgen Richter, *China: Enabling a New Era of Changes* (Singapore: John Wiley & Sons [Asia], 2003).

12. Ibid.

13. Nicholas R. Lardy, *China's Unfinished Economic Revolution* (Washington, DC: Brookings Institution Press, 1998).

14. The URC is funded by the central government, local government, and the company.

15. Fan Gang, "Reform and Development."

CHAPTER 3   Economic Forces at Work

1. Mark O'Neill, "Iraq Crisis Raises China Fears over Oil Security," *South China Morning Post*, September 19, 2002.

2. *CIA World Factbook*, 2005, www.odci.gov/cia/publications/factbook.

3. National Bureau of Statistics, China.

4. Ibid.

5. H. M. Hyndman, *Commercial Crises of the Nineteenth Century* (New York: Scribners, 1908).

6. Dan Denning, *The Bull Hunter* (New York: John Wiley & Sons, 2005).

7. Ibid.

8. Mark O'Neill, "China Fever Runs High among Executives Despite Dubious Statistics," *South China Morning Post*, December 2, 2002, online edition, wwwscmp.com.

9. Vincent Lim, "China Set to Strengthen Impressively in Technology Product Categories," *New Straits Times*, September 1, 2002, www.nst.com.

10. UNCTAD, *World Investment Report 2002: Transnational Corporations and Export Competitiveness*, 2002, www.unctad.org, accessed September 2005.

11. Hong Kong Trade Development Council, *Business Alert China*, November 15, 2002.

12. Andy Xie, "The IT Export Boom," September 27, 2002, cited from Pamela C. M. Mar and Frank-Jürgen Richter, *China: Enabling a New Era of Changes* (Singapore: John Wiley & Sons [Asia], 2003).

13. The four banks are the Agricultural Bank of China, Bank of China, China Construction Bank, and Industrial and Commercial Bank of China. Collectively, these four institutions are responsible for 67 percent of deposits and 60 percent of loans in China ("Moody's: Chinese Banking System's Outlook Stable," *Asian Banker Journal*, October 31, 2002).

14. "China's New Leaders Must Tackle Significant Economic Problems," AFX News Ltd., November 5, 2002, www.afxnews.com.

15. Pamela C. M. Mar and Frank-Jürgen Richter, *China: Enabling a New Era of Changes* (Singapore: John Wiley & Sons [Asia], 2003).

**CHAPTER 4 Emerging Investment Themes:
Global Supply and Demand**

1. Cesar Bacani, *The China Investor* (Singapore: John Wiley & Sons [Asia], 2003).

2. George Marshall, speech, June 5, 1946, cited at http://en .wikipedia.org, "Against Hunger, Bounty, Desperation, and Chaos," *Foreign Affairs*, May/June 1997.

3. Wu Xiaoling, "The Outlook for China's Monetary Policy," in Pamela C. M. Mar and Frank-Jürgen Richter, *China: Enabling a New Era of Changes* (Singapore: John Wiley & Sons [Asia], 2003).

4. Charles Mackay, *Extraordinary Popular Delusions and the Madness of Crowds*. New York: Harmony Books, 1980 (reprint from 1841 first edition).

5. Marc Faber, *Tomorrow's Gold* (Hong Kong: CLSA Books, 2003).

6. Martin S. Fridson, *It Was a Very Good Year* (New York: John Wiley & Sons, 1998).

7. Quoted in Elizabeth MacDonald, "Breaking Down the Numbers on Wall Street," *Forbes*, June 6, 2002.

8. Bernard Loomis, *International Tribune*, October 9, 1985.

9. Philip Bowring, "China 2002: The Geopolitical Context," in Pamela C. M. Mar and Frank-Jürgen Richter, *China: Enabling a New Era of Changes* (Singapore: John Wiley & Sons [Asia], 2003).

CHAPTER 5   Stock Markets, Domestic and International

1. Cesar Bacani, *The China Investor* (Singapore: John Wiley & Sons [Asia], 2003).

2. Standard & Poor's developed the concept of "core earnings" as earnings from a corporation's core business, and excluding non-recurring or noncore profits and losses. S&P uses these adjustments to rate bonds; however, investors improve their own analytical conclusions by making similar adjustments to earnings per share. The effect is substantial in many instances, drastically reducing reported profits and even wiping out profits to reflect a core-earnings-based net loss.

3. Bacani mentioned in his book the existence of at least two indexes focused on emerging corporations. These are the UBS China Private-Chip Index and the CLSA China Private Enterprise Index. There may be more in the future in the form of either index or ETF. One likely group of stocks worth tracking, for example, is the overall listings on Hong Kong's Growth Enterprise Market (GEM) exchange, and many ETFs for Hong Kong–listed company groupings are available.

4. Daniel Drew, in Richard J. Teweles and Edward S. Bradley, *The Stock Market*, 5th ed. (New York: John Wiley & Sons, 1987).

5. "Time to Close the Floor," www.webb-site.com, October 12, 2004.

6. Bacani, *China Investor.*

CHAPTER 6   An Investor's Road Map into China

1. Charles Gasparino and Susanne Craig, "Broker Watchdogs Face Scrutiny as Investor Complaints Mount," *Wall Street Journal*, May 23, 2002, p. 1; complaints statistics cited from National Association of Securities Dealers.
2. Deborah Solomon, "Salomon Draws Focus by SEC over Adelphia," *Wall Street Journal*, June 5, 2002, p. C1.
3. Jeff D. Opdyke, "Should You Trust Wall Street's New Ratings?," *Wall Street Journal*, July 17, 2002, p. D1; ratings analysis based on WSJ Research and First Call as of July 1, 2002.
4. Jeff D. Opdyke, "Stock Advice You Can Trust?," *Wall Street Journal*, October 31, 2002, p. D1.
5. "Americans Gloomy over Finances," Financial Planning Association press release, October 8, 2002.
6. International Accounting Standards (IAS), which are also the basis of Hong Kong Accounting Standards; U.S.-based GAAP; and China-based GAAP.
7. A similar full-disclosure system in the United States could include a three-part reporting of GAAP-based earnings; statutory earnings (what is reported for tax purposes); and core earnings (profit and loss from the corporation's core business, as well as core net worth reporting, a realistic evaluation of assets, liabilities, and net worth). Resistance to this idea comes from the fact that many U.S. companies cannot report their pension liabilities realistically without also admitting that they have negative net worth; this problem involves many companies such as General Motors and several U.S.-based airlines, among others.

CHAPTER 7   Developing a China Strategy

1. Investment Company Institute, 2005, www.ici.org.
2. Amy B. Crane, "e-Learning Series, Lesson 315," *BetterInvesting*, Value Line, 2002, www.betterinvesting.org.

3. Dustin Woodard, "Beware of 12b-1 Fees," online report at http://mutualfunds.about.com, accessed September 2005.
4. Michal Iachini, "Exchange-Traded Funds: Beyond the Hype," *Schwab Investing Insights*, March 17, 2005, www.investorguide .com.
5. Investment Company Institute, "Investment Exchange-Traded Fund Assets," July 2005.

CHAPTER 8   An Analysis of Chinese Stocks and Funds

1. Investment Company Institute and the U.S. Census Bureau, 2003.
2. Investment Company Institute, *2005 Investment Company Fact Book* (Washington, DC: Investment Company Institute, 2005).
3. Mergent Analysis, February 2006.
4. *China Securities Journal*, 2005.
5. Xinhua Finance, 2005.
6. Peter O'Shea, Mergent Analysis, 2006.

CHAPTER 9   The World of Tomorrow

1. International Monetary Fund (IMF), *World Economic Outlook Database*, April 2004, www.imf.org.
2. UNCTAD, *World Investment Report*, 2004, at www.unctad.org, accessed September 2005.
3. Pete Engardo and Dexter Roberts, "The China Price," *Business-Week*, December 6, 2004, www.businessweek.com.
4. *China Statistical Yearbook*, 2003; U.S. Commercial Service at www.buyusa.gov/china, accessed September 2005.
5. International Iron and Steel Institute, "World Steel in Figures," 2004, www.worldsteel.org, accessed September 2005.
6. Michael Elliott, "Small World, Big Stakes," *Time*, June 27, 2005, p. 30.
7. IMF, *World Economic Outlook Database*.

8. Automotive Resources Asia, BDAChina, Guangdong Kelon, SVA, Volkswagen, and Zoran; compiled in "China: Is the World Really Prepared?," Bernstein Investment Research and Management, Alliance Capital Management, 2004, p. 4.

9. Merrill Lynch, *The World Wealth Report*, 2004, at www.ml.com, accessed September 2005.

10. Based on population data from World Bank, "World Development Indicators," www.worldbank.org, accessed September 2005.

11. Jane Lanhee Lee, "GM Plans to Invest $3 Billion in China to Boost Its Presence," *Wall Street Journal*, June 7, 2004.

12. Bernstein Investment Research and Management, Alliance Capital Management, "China."

13. China Ministry of Information, Alliance Capital Management, Bernstein Investment Research and Management.

14. Shanghai Video & Audio, cited in Bernstein Investment Research and Management, "China," p. 8.

15. Broker estimates; Alliance Capital research, Bernstein Investment Research and Management, "China," p. 9.

16. National Bureau of Statistics, www.stats.gov.cn/English, accessed September 2005.

17. Ray Brooks and Ran Tao, "IMP Working Paper: China's Labor Market Performance and Challenges," November 2003.

18. Ibid.

19. Ibid.

20. *China Statistical Yearbook*, 2003.

21. World Bank, "World Development Indicators," September 2005, at www.worldbank.org.

22. Organization for Economic Cooperation and Development (OECD), "Main Science and Technology Indicators," 2003.

INDEX